Unveil the Mysteries of
THE FEMALE

THÉUN MARES

The Toltec Teachings Series:

Return of the Warriors

Cry of the Eagle

The Mists of Dragon Lore

This Darned Elusive Happiness

The Quest for Maleness

What people have been saying about Theun's work ...

"Required reading for anyone serious about really living life."

"I love his sense of humour and adaptability to everyday life situations."

"These books changed my life."

"I bought your book about four weeks ago now... what resulted was a "magical journey," which continues today."

Unveil the Mysteries of
THE FEMALE

THÉUN MARES

Lionheart
PUBLISHING

NOTE FROM THE AUTHOR

Those readers who are intending to read this book as well as *The Quest for Maleness*, should take note that the contents in many parts of these two books are more or less identical. This is necessarily so because of the nature of the material covered. Nonetheless, the wise reader will not be tempted to skip reading an apparent repeat, for although the content can be the same, the approach is nonetheless very different, and throws much light upon the more subtle differences between male and female.

ISBN 1-919792-06-6

Cover illustration by Tony Butler
DTP design by Mandy McKay
Printed and bound by Cape & Transvaal Book Printers, Parow, Cape.

Lionheart
PUBLISHING

Private Bag X5, Constantia 7848, Cape Town, South Africa
Phone: +27 21 794-4923
FAX: +27 21 794-1487
e-mail: lionheart@toltec-foundation.org
www.toltec-foundation.org
www.elusivehappiness.com

About the author

⛧

The author was born in Zimbabwe, of a mother who was a natural seer, and a father who was a miner. Having a seer's ability himself, Théun was trained from an early age in this art and in the disciplines of the Toltec tradition. Toltec means "A man or woman of knowledge," and the Toltec tradition encompasses a vast and ever-expanding system of knowledge about life, the universe and the part that we play within both.

Drawing upon his knowledge of the fundamental unity of all of life, the author has used his seer's skills and training to uncover the essential truths that lie at the heart of all true religions and belief systems. In his books, he reveals the nature of these core truths, which have so often become distorted, corrupted and lost with the passage of time. He also shows how we can use these truths in a practical manner to revolutionize our thinking, our behaviour and our world.

The author's career has spanned the breadth of the performing arts, education and business. He now lives in Cape Town with Marianne, where he divides his time between writing, teaching and creating courses for adults and teenagers.

The overall aim of Théun's work is firstly, to rekindle in all of us the knowledge that the whole purpose of life is the evolution of awareness, and secondly, to imbue in us an understanding of how this is best achieved.

His message is that the only possible way for us to create a hope-filled future, rather than a world filled with destruction, is by developing the openness of heart to embrace all of life fully, instead of becoming separative, divisive and indulging in escapisms.

Embracing all of life involves meeting all our challenges head-on, rather than running away from them. It involves developing and maintaining respect for the world in which we live, and for life in general; it involves acknowledging that all our actions have an impact on those around us, and it also involves the constant willingness to respond – to take action – based upon the feedback we are getting from our lives. Introversion only implies cutting ourselves off from life.

The overall import of Théun's message is that, in the final analysis, the proper evolution of awareness can only come about as a result of practical experience. Wasting time in philosophizing, intellectualizing, rationalizing and escapisms only serve to lead one further and further away from practical experience, and from the real business of living. For the only thing of lasting value in life upon the physical plane is to live it all, to experience it all, to embrace it all: the good with the bad, and so to develop the sense of utter inclusiveness, which is the mark of a passionate, alive, and truly human, being with a heart.

Table of Contents

To Marianne, the most magical female I have ever known, and to Elizabeth, Dawn, Moya, Ursula, Inge and Louise, who are all exceptional ladies. To share my life and the Warrior's Path with Marianne is my special privilege, and to observe whilst each of these ladies unfolds her mystifying potential as a female is uniquely uplifting and joyous.

Preface

Dear Ladies,

On being requested by Théun to write the preface for this book, I was confronted by feelings familiar to all of us. Excitement, at the possibility inherent within the nascent, and fear, at having to expose my capabilities in the face of an unknown domain, namely writing. As with many life situations I had a choice, either to be guided by my excitement or allow my fear to debilitate me.

True to being female, I chose excitement for my guide.

As females you will be able to identify with this choice. But all too often we allow our hearts to be overridden by our minds or logic, negating an intuitive knowing. By doing so, we abandon the vitality and spontaneity so natural to the female. Succumbing to this pattern of behaviour, we wilfully trade what it means to be a female for the male's logic and end up becoming either second–rate males, or doormats.

You, as the reader, will have to make similar choices when reading this book, because many of the concepts concerning what it means to be female may at first glance appear weird and contradictory.

But if you allow your intuitive knowledge to guide you, you will enter a whole new world.

In order to navigate through this new world you will need to honestly acknowledge what you already know, trust in your abilities as a female and believe in your innate potential.

Just as a child entering Grade 4 acknowledges that she has passed Grade 3 and must therefore trust in her abilities to pass Grade 4, so too must she believe that she can do it.

Having arrived in this world as a female your potential is your femininity. You may ask, what is femininity? Observing women in your own life you will easily see what femininity is not.

For it is not: the dominant woman who treats her husband or male partner as she would a child, believing she can do anything better than a man; the little girl: those women who continually feign helplessness as a guise for manipulation; the prima donna: those women who through their self-centredness attach importance only to outer appearances; the corporate business executive: those women who believe that women are inferior to men and that they need to compete against them.

Being female means having the courage to stand with dignity and to present the equal but opposite polarity for the male in her life.

This book represents a map or set of departure points from where you can begin to unfold your own journey towards your femininity. In the game of life, as in any other game, we do not proceed from novice to champion overnight.

Nonetheless, if we learn to embrace the triumphs and the setbacks, we can experience all the richnesses life has to offer.

So, if you are willing to be courageous and to listen to your heart, your journey will be exciting, fulfilling and magical.

I wish you well on this wonderful adventure.

Marianne.

Introduction

❦

By today's standards, the material contained in this book is highly controversial and flies in the face of most of Western society's accepted norms and beliefs regarding the sexes. Consequently you are advised to consider what follows with the sort of openness of mind, even if only partial or temporary, that will enable you to achieve an approach that is unbiased and which contains three vital ingredients.

First, you must convince yourself that, by virtue of simply being alive, you are a unique person with a special task in life, and that being female is part of that uniqueness. Second, you must want to read this book because you desire to find out more about the mystery which is you; and third, you must be honest enough to accept that maybe everything you think you know about being a female could be wrong.

To express it differently, if you think you are nothing special, and have nothing of importance to accomplish in this life, then this book is not for you. Rather give it to a friend whom you think is special and important, and try to find yourself some other book that deals with something like doormats or martyrs. Likewise, if you believe that there is nothing mysterious about you, and that you already know everything about being female, then this book is also not for you. Throw it away. This book is definitely not for people who are boring stereotypes of the heavily socially-conditioned masses. Instead this book is for the woman who has enough self-respect and sense of adventure to want to stand out as being unique and special. The fashionable trend amongst women today, to descend to the same dishonourable mediocrity as everyone else, may well excite some, but it does nothing for the true female. Knowing in her heart of hearts that to be a true female means setting the trend, rather than following it, and dictating the fashion, rather than submitting to it, the true female looks upon the female masses with sympathy, if not with downright pity!

This book has been written for those women who are proud of being females, and who therefore wish to set their own trends and dictate their own fashions. For women such as these, to end up wearing the same dress as another woman is regrettable, but to be expected to subscribe to another woman's ideas is an unthinkable outrage! These are the females who agree amongst themselves on one issue only, namely, that to be female is a high honour and a privilege that is unique in its quality to every female. Therefore, only by disagreeing with each other can they stand together in safeguarding and preserving the uniqueness and the specialness that comprises each of them! These are the females who cause every male to catch his breath when she walks into the room, and to shake his head in utter bewilderment when, after laughing politely at his compliments, she pats his arm reassuringly before suddenly turning her attentions to someone else in the room, be it another male eager to please, or a female rival showing her claws by straightening her hair or skirts and baring her teeth in an overly-polite greeting. Such females make every other woman wish that she had, as a girl, paid more attention to the meaning of being a woman, rather than trying to outdo the boys.

If you are really going to benefit from this book, you must have committment – committment to yourself, and committment to that mystery which spells female. If you are not committed, the wrong patterns will persist, and unless you change the patterns of your behaviour, how are you ever going to change anything in your life? What will help you greatly in maintaining your committment is to bear in mind, throughout this book, that there are rules made by men and women, and there are rules imposed upon us by fate. Most women follow only the rules of society, even if they believe themselves to be free-thinking individuals. But to adhere to fashion, or to join the ranks of those who are pushing a new and fashionable concept, is merely to subscribe to social conditioning, and therefore to follow the rules of society. The true female, who acknowledges the fact that she is unique, and therefore special, does not subscribe to such prejudices and preconceived ideas. Having a hidden agenda all of her own, the true female pursues her own individuality and, like the Mona Lisa, smiles quietly at the naive attempts of feminist movements trying their damndest to deny their own femininity in the cause of femininity! Like all members of her sex, the true female can at times be highly irrational, but unlike most other women, she is most certainly never illogical!

Being a male, and therefore from a purely male perspective, I offer this book to all true females as a salute to their ineffable quality of mystery – a mystery which not only enthrals and excites, but which also calls forth strongly the masculine desire to unveil that mystery.

Always a paradox. Always tangible, but also, somehow, elusive and just out of reach. Always present, and yet, somehow, removed, the true female seems for ever, strangely, inexplicably, a wonderful and unfathomable mystery! How utterly sad it is that the majority of women today are so denying their own femininity in pursuit of female liberation, that they are inadvertently trading that mystery for the fashionable concept of sexual equality. If women need to be liberated, then it is not that they need to be liberated from what it means to be a female, but rather that they need to be liberated from the popular belief that to be a female somehow means to be inferior to the male, and that it is therefore an unfortunate quirk of fate to have been born a living mystery. Perhaps this book will do at least something towards correcting that terrible lie, and towards restoring to the true female the acknowledgement which she so justly deserves, as well as the honour which has always been her divine birthright by virtue of the awe she inspires in every male.

PART ONE

The mystery of gender

CHAPTER 1

Entering the world of the female

❦

Having discarded the obvious in favour of
intellectual complexity, men and women have lost touch
with their feelings, including those feelings that
pertain to the mystery of gender.

No one can tell you how to become a female, for every female is unique. Other women can tell you what being female means to them, but how is that going to help you when you are not the same as them? Men can tell you what they think women should be, but being men, they can no more teach you to be a female than a bird can teach a fish to fly! So, if you would like to enter the world of the true female, you must first learn what that world is, and then you must learn how to claim it, how to make it your own. This may sound like a complicated riddle, but it is in fact simplicity itself. Why? The secret lies in coming to the realisation that you do not have to go anywhere in search of anything, for the simple reason that you are already there, wherever "there" may be, and you already have everything you need, whatever "everything" may mean to you.

However, before we can learn what the world of the true female is, we must understand first of all that, from a certain perspective, the terms "male" and "female" pertain to specific states of awareness, and secondly that any awareness we have is something we bring about within ourselves. This last point is particularly important when it comes to considering our sexual identity. Because you were born a woman, you have a specific gender, rather than being an "it." In practical terms this means that you are at the opposite polarity to men, and not some sort of asexual oddity that falls somewhere in-between the two poles.

So, from a very basic level, there is your body, which is that of a woman, and there is the you who indwells that body, possessing an awareness which is built up around your physical gender. This awareness of yours is of course not limited or, at least, it shouldn't be. You can develop your awareness to any level you choose, and in any direction you choose. The possible development of your awareness is what, for the purposes of this book, we will define as your potential.

The word "potential" comes from the root "potent," meaning your ability, or power. So in talking about potential, we are talking about your inner abilities and power, which you may or may not be aware of, and which you have perhaps never explored. It is therefore for the sake of clarity, and not prejudice, that we define the potential in women as femininity, as opposed to masculinity, which is the potential in men.

Following on from our definition, we arrive at the fact that you are a being indwelling a body which has the physical gender termed woman, you have an awareness termed female, and you have a potential which is termed femininity. So, to want to develop

17

> ### THE WORLD OF THE FEMALE
>
> = *A STATE OF AWARENESS*
> *which you must learn how*
> *to claim and make YOUR OWN*
>
> | | | |
> |---|---|---|
> | *Woman* | = | *Gender = Your own physical body* |
> | *Female* | = | *Your awareness* |
> | *Femininity* | = | *Your potential* |

any potential other than your own is to deny yourself your own potential, and what good is that? Yet it is crazy to see how many women are trying to become males, and vice versa, all in the name of sexual equality. If we were meant to be unisexual, then surely we would have been born hermaphrodites! It just doesn't make sense that men and women are trying to become an "it," when they have a potential that is clearly feminine or masculine.

The purpose of this book is firstly to give you real tools to put you in touch with your own feelings concerning femininity, and secondly, to provide you with information that will enable you to use those feelings to unfold your potential as a female. More than this I cannot do, and neither can anyone else for that matter, whatever claims or promises he or she may make. This is because no-one can give you an awareness of what it is to be female – all of us have to claim our knowledge for and by ourselves. Yet specific tools and select information can be invaluable for helping you discover the true nature of the world of the female, and how you can make it your own.

Life is not an intellectual process.

Life is a feeling.

CHAPTER TWO

Getting to grips with your potential

❧❧❧

*In dealing with mystery it is wise to bear in
mind that one is up against the unknown. Only fools
are so ignorant as to want to fake cleverness in the
face of the unknown. The wise ones are sufficiently
humble to allow their feelings to guide them.*

If we are to come to grips with the mystery of the
female, we need to acquire at least a rudimentary
understanding of that baffling secret we term the
evolution of awareness. However, the scope of this book does not
allow for us to become too involved in technicalities that are
enough to stretch even the ablest of minds to their limits.
Therefore, if you would like a deeper insight into these areas of
teaching, my first series of books will throw considerable light
upon a subject which we are here going to gloss over very,
very superficially.

Now, before we can look at what it means to be a female, we
need to go back to another point which is so obvious that most
people simply ignore it. In fact we have already touched upon
this point, namely, that all of us are basically spirit beings

indwelling a physical body. For the purposes of this book I am going to use the terminology of my own particular training, although, of course, you can use whatever terminology makes sense to you. What I am going to try to do is simply to sketch out for both of us a common meeting ground so that we will understand each other.

From my perspective, which is similar to that of most of the great world religions, man is primarily a spirit being who comes into incarnation. Now whether you wish to believe that this happens only once, or whether you wish to believe in reincarnation, doesn't actually matter. Whatever you choose to believe, one way or another the spirit being, that is, you, comes into incarnation. However, it is not that the spirit being itself comes into incarnation, but rather that its *awareness* comes to indwell a physical body on the physical plane. Toltecs term this incarnating awareness *the dreamer*, but we do not need to get hung up on terminology. If you prefer, you can term this the soul, or the reincarnating ego, or the higher self, or whatever else you like, as long as you understand what I mean by *the dreamer*. Remember that it is essentially the *awareness* of a being we are referring to at this point.

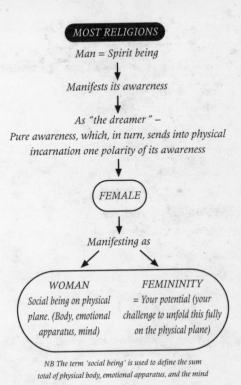

MOST RELIGIONS

Man = Spirit being

Manifests its awareness

As "the dreamer" –
Pure awareness, which, in turn, sends into physical
incarnation one polarity of its awareness

FEMALE

Manifesting as

WOMAN
Social being on physical
plane. (Body, emotional
apparatus, mind)

FEMININITY
= Your potential (your
challenge to unfold this fully
on the physical plane)

NB The term 'social being' is used to define the sum
total of physical body, emotional apparatus, and the mind

What you should always keep in mind regarding this awareness, i.e., the dreamer, is that the term "female" refers to the one polarity of its existence, whereas the term "male" refers to its other polarity. This means that whenever we speak about female, we are referring to a specific polarity of the dreamer's awareness, and not to the female body as such. Your physical body is simply an expression of your feminine potential, and it is this physical expression which we term "woman." Clearly, what this implies is that you, the spirit being, have already incarnated one polarity of your awareness upon the physical plane by taking upon yourself a physical body termed "woman." Further, that one polarity of your awareness is not just what we term "female," since it also has a potential which is feminine by nature. From all this it stands to reason that the whole purpose of incarnating is to unfold or to develop your potential or, in other words, to unfold your full awareness of what it is to be female.

This is the same thing as saying that to be a true female implies that you are manifesting your full potential, which is feminine, upon the physical plane, as a woman. If this sounds overly obvious, as it should, then have a good look around you. Out of all the thousands of women you can see, how many would you term true females? Would you call yourself a true female?

TRUE FEMALE
↓
*You as a woman bringing
out your full potential*
↓
= Femininity

CHAPTER THREE

The origin of gender

*Locked within the secret of gender lie the
keys to evolution. The man or woman who has
mastered the secret of gender has unlimited
power at his or her command.*

In the previous chapter we saw that the terms
"male" and "female" refer to the two polarities of
our awareness, and that through the act of incarnation we manifest either of these two polarities in terms of
manhood or womanhood. The implication of all this is, naturally,
that every woman has an inner male counterpart, and that every
man has an inner female counterpart, since these are the
opposite polarities of our incarnated awareness.

With respect to the nature of these two polarities, the male
represents the spirit of man, and the female represents the
physical being, that is, the incarnation, of man. (By the term
"man" I am referring to those spirit beings broadly referred to as
mankind). Toltecs term these two polarities the *nagal* (pronounced na-hal) and the *tonal* respectively, and it is through the

interaction between these two polarities that the evolution of awareness takes place. Therefore we have:

MALE   =   NAGAL (the spirit of man)

FEMALE   =   TONAL (the physical being)

In case you are already thinking that this smacks too much of sexual inequality, let me explain a little more. First, remember that we are all spirit beings in physical incarnation and, as a result, all of us, irrespective of gender, have a nagal and a tonal. Second, remember also that in speaking of male and female we are referring to states of awareness, and that all awareness is relative to other states of awareness, irrespective of whether the actual physical manifestation of that awareness is masculine or feminine in gender. In *This Darned Elusive Happiness* I explained the relative factor of awareness, but for our present understanding we now need to look a little more deeply at what this actually implies. To do so, let us consider the grand scheme of things.

If we look at life in its totality, we keep coming back to that age-old question: "What am I?" Although we have already answered this question, we still do not really know what our answer means. Clearly, this is a type of question we can only partially answer, in that all we can safely say about ourselves is what we know ourselves to be in physical terms. Therefore rather than try to answer a question that lies beyond our present capability of answering, let us rather ask the question in such a way that we can answer it, if only in part. Thus the real question is: "What is this *me* termed the tonal?" or: "What is this *me* termed the physical being?"

This *me* which is the physical being, the tonal, has, as we all know, a physical body which is not only capable of sensory perception, but through which it is also possible to perceive in terms of emotional responses, as well as mental impulses. This is the physical plane manifestation of ourselves. But is this all there is to us? Although many materialists and atheists will argue that this is so, no-one in his right mind can really agree with such a simplistic definition of man. If we care to think only just a little further than our noses, we very quickly come to realise that somewhere "inside" of us is an indwelling being that not only controls our physical body, but also our emotions and our thoughts. Yet, who is that inner being? That inner being is what we have termed our awareness, that part of our dreamer that is in incarnation. I say "that part of" because the total dreamer is the total awareness of the spirit being, but remember that during incarnation the spirit being manifests only one polarity of its awareness in terms of manhood or womanhood.

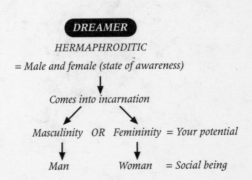

DREAMER

HERMAPHRODITIC

= Male and female (state of awareness)

Comes into incarnation

Masculinity OR Femininity = Your potential

Man   Woman   = Social being

There are many different ways in which we can view the tonal, but for the purposes of this book we are going to look at only one of these definitions. Essentially the tonal is *every-thing* we know ourselves to be, for even that part of our awareness which controls our physical body, emotions and thoughts, must also be part of the tonal, or incarnated being. Of the other polarity of our awareness, and of the spirit being itself, we know nothing. Therefore, for the sake of clarity, we term the tonal *every-thing*, and we term the spirit being, which is the nagal, *no-thing*, simply because from our angle as physical beings the spirit is nothing we know. Thus we have:

NAGAL　　=　　NO-THING

TONAL　　=　　EVERY-THING

What is implied in the above is quite obvious, namely, that the tonal is life in manifestation, whilst the nagal is life unmanifest.

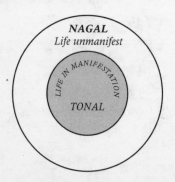

MAN = SPIRIT BEING

NAGAL/SPIRIT = MASCULINE

      ↑
     INTERACTION
      ↓

              = No body, emotions
                 or mental ability
              = Nothing

   TONAL   *= FEMININE*

              = Social being
              = Body and emotions
                 and mental faculties
              = Everything

* The interaction between spirit and tonal, masculine and feminine, leads to the evolution of awareness

This brings us back to the concept of potential, for clearly the sole purpose of manifestation is to unfold potential, i.e., the spirit incarnates as a result of wanting to explore its own potential. Therefore not only is the spirit the source of all manifested life, but it also pervades the whole of manifested life. Keeping this as simple as possible, we say that the spirit manifests so as to get to know aspects of itself which it does not yet know, namely, its potential. However, in order to do this, it has to separate the known from the unknown. This means that the spirit has to separate that which it knows about itself from that which it does not yet know.

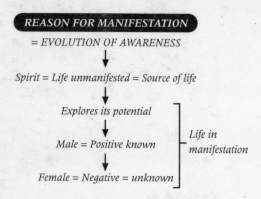

That which is the known implies knowledge which can be utilised, and is like having money in the bank - having a positive bank balance. On the other hand, that which is unknown is like one's potential earnings, which, being only potential, cannot be used until they have been materialised in some way and have been incorporated into one's bank account. This is much like pulling off a business deal so as to earn extra income - until such time as that deal has paid off in terms of hard cash, the potential income from the deal is exactly that, namely, potential. Therefore if the known is like a positive bank balance, then relative to the known, the unknown is as yet negative, meaning that it is still pending. Thus we have:

KNOWN = POSITIVE

UNKNOWN = NEGATIVE

Now just like any good businessman, the spirit also wants to expand its business, (which is the evolution of awareness), to its maximum potential, in that the spirit wishes to include the unknown within the known. However, remember that the physical being, or the tonal, is in fact every-thing, in that it represents all aspects of manifested life, and therefore it must by definition be both chaos and order, light and darkness, positive and negative, male and female. But clearly, if the evolution of awareness is to proceed intelligently, then even at this level it is necessary for the spirit to separate one polarity from the other. It is this act of separation that gives rise to what Toltecs refer to as *the splitting of the sexes*. Yet in relation to all of this we are still only referring to existence at the level of pure awareness – the awareness of the spirit being.

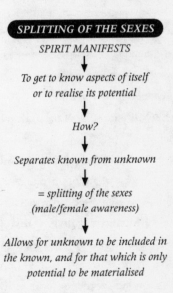

SPLITTING OF THE SEXES

SPIRIT MANIFESTS

↓

*To get to know aspects of itself
or to realise its potential*

↓

How?

↓

Separates known from unknown

↓

*= splitting of the sexes
(male/female awareness)*

↓

*Allows for unknown to be included in
the known, and for that which is only
potential to be materialised*

So, it is therefore not a question of one aspect being more important than the other. It is simply a question of having to separate one pole from the other, for the evolution of awareness to proceed unencumbered. Within this process it is also clear why it should be the known that guides and directs the course of evolution, for how else could it be? If the spirit being did not separate the known from the unknown, and then use what it does know in order to unfold more awareness, how could evolution take place? How can we run a business on money we do not have? Therefore when we state that the known is positive relative to the unknown, we are also implying that the tonal is dependent upon the spirit being, not only for incarnation, but also for direction within the course of evolution. To clarify this further let us revert once again to our analogy of owning a business.

If you have your own business, the existence of that business is thanks to you. Without you your business would not exist. Your business is entirely dependent upon the time, the effort and the money you invest in it. The reason why you invest in this business is because it has a great potential, but unless you use your knowledge, unless you use what you know, in order to develop your business, the business will fail. Therefore look upon your business as being the tonal, in which case you are the nagal. Because you are the directing force within that business, you are positive relative to the business.

From this analogy we can see how, because of the way in which life works, the tonal is negative relative to the nagal, and why it is also looked upon as being feminine relative to the nagal. Why feminine? Simply because just as it is the male who carries and secretes the life-giving sperm, so too is it the spirit who carries and "secretes" the purpose of life. Without that purpose, without that "sperm," there would be no conception, no birth, and therefore no manifestation or incarnation. This is equally true of you the businesswoman, for although, relative to your business, you are the male, and even though you direct that business with your sense of purpose, unless you also conceive it and bring it to birth, and continue to nurture it, there will be no business.

It can of course always be argued that there is no reason why it cannot be the female who provides the purpose, but consider how illogical such an argument really is. Have you ever heard of or encountered anyone who was brought to birth by a business, and whose very existence was then determined by that business? Such an argument is absurd, and is invariably the sign of a distorted mind that upholds the concept of sexual inequality. Although it is true that many people do become the product of their businesses, that is not their origin, and the behaviour of such people is as contrary to the natural order of life as is the behaviour of those who persist in practising sexual inequality. Even you as the businesswoman do not provide the purpose of your business. You merely direct your business according to a purpose you can sense – a purpose provided by your own inner spirit which is the true male in your life upon the physical plane.

From what we have looked at so far, it should not be difficult to see that because the female is negative relative to the spirit, she by definition constitutes for the spirit the unknown which, as we have already noted, is in reality its potential. This potential is of course manifested life, the tonal, and since the tonal is everything, light and darkness, male and female, the spirit must of necessity separate one polarity from the other. The end result of this separation is what we term a physical being that is either a man or a woman, and that has an awareness which is either male or female, and a potential for either masculinity or femininity.

If we look at how things work at the level of the physical plane, we find that the physical being termed "woman" is also negative relative to the physical being termed "man." This is because she has the same relationship to man as female awareness has to male awareness. However, since they are negative, all women are in a very real sense a mixture of order and chaos, light and darkness, male and female, and it is herein that the mystery of the female lies. The mystery is centred around the fact that the female is, in essence, all of these things, for, as the representative of the tonal, she is every-thing. This does not mean that the female is some sort of freak. Instead it means that the female has a completely different configuration to the male, in that, unlike the male, the female has two distinct sides to her.

As we progress with our study of the female we will look at what this really means, but for now understand that it is this mystery which constitutes for the spirit the unknown. So, from the angle of the male, who is the representative of the spirit, the female is very much a mystery. In fact, if the truth be told, the female is equally a mystery unto herself, even though, generally speaking, women do not like to acknowledge this.

MYSTERY OF THE FEMALE (AWARENESS)

TONAL = EVERYTHING
= All of manifested life

Both

Chaos	&	Order
Light	&	Dark
Positive	&	Negative

Summing up all of the above, we find that all of us are spirit beings with an awareness termed the dreamer. That awareness has two polarities, termed male and female. Therefore, at this level of existence we are all hermaphrodites. However, in order to unfold our full potential we need to evolve our awareness, and in order to do so we have to separate the known from the unknown. This brings about the splitting of the sexes and, as a result, and depending upon what our approach to unfolding our potential is to be, we incarnate either the male-side or the female-side of our awareness.

If it is the male-side, then we have a man's body and we approach life from the angle of the spirit, that is, the known. If it is the female-side, then we have a woman's body and we approach life from the angle of the tonal, that is, the unknown. However, in working with the unknown, it is important to remember that until it has been incorporated into the known, it must of necessity be potential. And in being a potential, it is by nature every-thing, positive and negative, light and darkness, male and female, just as within any business there is the potential for both success and failure. Consequently, although as spirit beings we have no physical gender as such, being both male and female, if we wish to unfold our full potential, we must manifest that potential. This means that we must incarnate onto the physical plane. In doing so we effect the splitting of the sexes, with the result that we incarnate either as male or female.

If we are male, then it is a simple splitting into the known and the unknown. However, if we are female, then that splitting in a sense remains undifferentiated and is still the unknown. As I have already mentioned, how all of this really works is far too technical for the purposes of this book, but with at least this very simplistic understanding of the concept of gender we can now begin to work consciously with the mystery of the female. Therefore let it suffice for now to say that if we give to the unknown the value of X, and we give to the known the value of Y, then during the splitting of the sexes the male is determined by XY, whereas the female is determined by XX, a fact which is reflected in the sex chromosomes.

The implications of this are enormous, and they amount to the fact that, unless the proper interaction between males and females takes place, the evolution of awareness does not proceed intelligently and we end up with the kind of mess we see in the world today. Because the unknown is a mystery, and will always remain so, the mystey of the female can never be fully solved. Yet, through the co-operation between male and female, the unknown can gradually become incorporated into the known. Only in this way can men achieve their full potential of masculinity, and can women achieve their full potential of femininity.

In practical terms this means that the mystery of the female can never be solved, or the potential of the female can never be realised, unless she can be incorporated into the purpose, and therefore also the life, of the male. This is because it is the male which constitutes the known, and therefore also order.

In working to realise her full potential, the female co-operates with, or assists, the male firstly, by providing him with a counterbalance; secondly, by complementing him in every respect; and thirdly, by supporting him in claiming his power. We will shortly be looking at what this actually means, but we first need to explore the dual nature of the female.

CHAPTER FOUR

The dual nature of the female

~~~~~~~~~~

We have already seen that the female is essentially both order and chaos, light and darkness, positive and negative, male and female. Toltecs refer to this dual nature of the female in terms of the mother and the female. Since a mother, as a result of the relative factor of awareness, is masculine relative to her children, irrespective of their gender, Toltecs term the male in the female the mother, and term the female in her simply the female.

In any relationship the female can play either the role of the mother, or the role of the true female, and this includes her relationship with men. So, if you are a businesswoman and you run your own business, then it is the mother in you, which is masculine in quality, that is running your business. Likewise, if you are a married woman, but find that it is you who has to make all the decisions, then once again it is the mother in you who is keeping the marriage together. However, realise what this implies, especially in your marriage. Quite simply, it means that if you are in mother mode within your marriage, then you do not have a husband, but a son. From your husband's perspective he does not have a wife, but a mother to whom he is like a little boy.

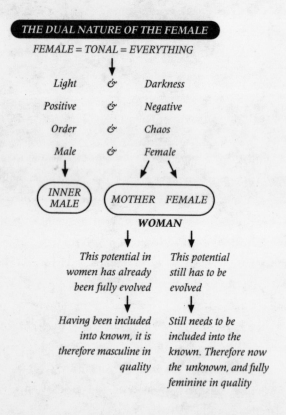

THE DUAL NATURE OF THE FEMALE

FEMALE = TONAL = EVERYTHING

Light	*&*	*Darkness*
Positive	*&*	*Negative*
Order	*&*	*Chaos*
Male	*&*	*Female*

INNER MALE **MOTHER FEMALE**

WOMAN

This potential in women has already been fully evolved	*This potential still has to be evolved*
Having been included into known, it is therefore masculine in quality	*Still needs to be included into the known. Therefore now the unknown, and fully feminine in quality*

The situation described above is by far the biggest cause of unhappiness and problems within most marriages, because sooner or later the woman begins to tire of having to mother her husband and to have sex with her son, and the man, in his turn, also begins to tire of constantly being told what to do, including when and how to make love to his mother!

The possible results of such a situation are almost unlimited. For example, the husband can start to have affairs with younger women who are less likely to want to mother him, or his wife, for that matter, can start to have affairs with men whom she feels she does not have to mother. The couple can become estranged, or divorced. The man can become aggressive in wanting to dominate his wife as he attempts to assert his maleness, even to the point of becoming violent. The woman can become even more domineering in her efforts to get her husband to enact his true role as the male, with the result that the marriage either deteriorates completely, or the man erupts into physical violence, or just withdraws more and more into himself, becoming evermore the little boy. But in most cases, the problem arises because the man is not fulfilling his true function as the male, with the result that the female is forced into the role of the mother.

CHAPTER FIVE

Separating myth from reality

*Although ignorance begets myth, we cannot
afford to forget that all reality is masked by myth.
Therefore care must be taken not to discard the
baby with the bathwater.*

f you look at yourself, and then at every woman around you, you will quickly see that precious little of what you think you know about what it means to be a female is what you may rightfully claim as being your own knowledge, gained through your own experience. In fact, if you really want to be honest with yourself, you will have to admit that most of what we think we know about ourselves is based entirely upon two things; the first relating to our physical existence; and the second concerning the information fed to us through our social conditioning.

Think for a moment. Who and what are you? Realise that you are not your name. Your name only serves to identify you by virtue of the fact that you have a physical body. If you did not have a physical body you would not have a name, neither would you be a woman, a wife, a mother, a teacher, or anything else. However, you are not your body! As we saw earlier, neither are you your thoughts or emotions, because you can control all of these.

Regarding the second point, we can equally see that none of the information we have been fed through our social conditioning does anything towards informing us about who and what we really are. All of this information is based entirely upon other people's perceptions and beliefs, which mostly have their basis in misconception and prejudice. What's more, the sole purpose of being fed this information is to condition all of us, firstly, into accepting the prejudices of others; and secondly, into having to conform to the biased actions of the majority. The rationale here being that the majority must be right, and the individual must be wrong, unless he or she conforms with what the majority wants.

Consequently, if we are going to get to grips with what is entailed within the mystery of gender and, more specifically, if you are going to grasp what it means to be a true female, then we are going to have to sift through everything we think we know, in order to be able to separate myth from reality. I say sift, because it is important to bear in mind that everything, even the most outrageous fantasies, at some time had the basis of their origins in reality. Because of this we cannot afford simply to discard everything we know, as a result of the anger we feel at having been conditioned into accepting the lies, the prejudices and the misconceptions of others, for in amongst all of that trash lie the kernels of truth we are seeking.

Nevertheless, I must warn you that in our attempts at separating reality from myth, you will many times find yourself wanting to resist the concepts we come up with. The reason for this is that we are dealing here with the result of a great many generations of suppression, of inequality, of injustice and of the suffering and struggle of women the world over to try to free themselves from that humiliation. In view of this, it will all too often appear as if I am trying to force women back into the very suppression from which they are only just beginning to escape. However, I am not trying to force women back in time. If you will bear with me, then hopefully, as the contents of this book unfold, you will begin to see that far from trying to suppress the female, I am doing everything I can to ensure her liberation, and to accord to her the acknowledgement and the respect she has been denied for so very long.

I must also point out that we cannot possibly address every myth and every issue in this book. Accordingly, I have selected only the nine most commonly-held myths. But if we look at these in depth, we will soon come to see that they are in fact the source of all other myths. By addressing these basic nine myths we can gain the necessary insight to enable us to unravel any other myth, by virtue of the fact that all myths have their origins in one or another of the basic nine premises.

PART TWO

The nine myths and their hidden keys

CHAPTER SIX

MYTH ONE
Women are weak

❧

*T*here are a great many different interpretations given to this myth, most of which have nothing to do with the truth. The real meaning of this myth is that the female is negative relative to the male. As we have already noted, this does not mean that the woman is inferior to the male, but that the male and the female are equal but opposite polarities of the dreamer. If we look further, into the deeper implications inherent within this myth, we discover that because the female is negative relative to the male, not only does she provide the male with a counterbalance, but she complements him in every respect. In this way, the female supports the male in claiming his power. Consequently, far from meaning that the female is literally weak, the term "weak" refers to the role she is playing in the life of the male. In order to grasp this let us consider each of these points in more detail.

What does it mean to provide the male with a counterbalance? Because the female is negative, she will quite often see things very differently to the male. Therefore instead of always just agreeing with the male, the true female will express to the male her point of view, should it be different to his.

This does not imply that the female purposefully and deliberately disagrees with everything the male says, but simply that the female's opinion adds a different perspective to what the male already knows. However, even though her own opinion may indeed be different to that of the male, this does not mean that the female is necessarily disagreeing with him, as so many men are only too eager to believe. By showing the male a different perspective, the female is in fact making it possible for him to break any fixation he may have, as a result perhaps of having become too focussed on the issue at hand.

There are always many ways in which a situation can be viewed. But, because the male is the hunter, he naturally tends to be very focussed on his prey, with the result that he can become so one-pointed in his way of thinking that he will quite often stare himself blind at a problem. The reason for this is that, in focussing, the male's vision becomes locked into the task at hand, and so he becomes fixated. However, once one is fixated, it is no longer possible to see other avenues of approach. An example will help to make all of this somewhat clearer.

Pierre is not happy in his work, and is therefore excited when he is offered a new business opportunity with John, a friend of his. However, in discussing the possible new venture with his wife, Cindy, Pierre notices that although Cindy is listening to him attentively, she does not seem to be as excited as he is. When Pierre asks her about her apparent lack of enthusiasm, Cindy points out to him that she feels very uncomfortable about the proposal, not because the proposal is bad, but because of the person who made it.

Thinking about what Cindy has said, Pierre remembers that he has often in the past not felt sure that he could always depend on John. Being an impulsive man, given to making rash promises so as to get the approval of others, John all-too-often makes himself guilty of not keeping his word. Yet, through being so focussed on finding himself another job, Pierre overlooked this point when John made the proposal.

In this example it is easy to see how Cindy helped her husband to achieve a greater and more balanced perspective on John's offer. But the real meaning of the female providing the male with a counterbalance goes even deeper than this. The male, generally speaking, will always focus on the potential for the positive, because it is his aim to hunt down his prey. Therefore if, as in Pierre's case, he is looking for a new job, and he finds something that he likes, he will tend to concentrate on acquiring that job without necessarily looking at all the unexpected circumstances that could accompany the job. Naturally, it is not only new jobs we are talking about here, but everything in the life of the male, be it a new house, a holiday, a mistress, a mental ideal, or even a pet habit!

The female, on the other hand, because her nature is to preserve and to protect, is not only cautious, but also suspicious in her approach. As a result, the female is always on the look-out for the negative, and so is also quick to smell a rat. However, this is a natural characteristic of the true female that flies in the face of our social conditioning, and it therefore often lands the female in a great deal of trouble, in the sense of her being accused of pessimism, of being nasty and vindictive, or simply of being a bitch. It is sad to see how often a man will angrily accuse his wife of being pessimistic, instead of supporting him in his ideas and his attempts. And yet it is never the true female's intention to undermine the male's belief in himself. The only thing she is trying to do is to give him her perspective on the negative.

The true male will always welcome the female perspective. Far from making him insecure, it instead makes him even more confident, in that it allows him to look at the situation from both polarities. Therefore rather than being angered by the female's negativity, the true male will always encourage the female to give him her input, and, if the woman is a true female, she will try to point out to him everything that she perceives could possibly turn out to be negative. Because none of us can think or decide for another person, although the female gives the male her input, the final decision is still his. But if the male values the female's input, he will always take her perspective into account in making his decision.

So many relationships go wrong simply because this intelligent co-operation, which should be practised between the male and the female, is being ignored. Out of the many reasons why people do not practise intelligent co-operation, the principal one is insecurity.

Often, for whatever reason, the man does not really believe in his ability as a hunter and a provider, and so he feels insecure in his role as the male. This insecurity will generally manifest in one of two ways. The first way is for the man to become highly defensive about his ideas whenever his wife expresses something negative, in which case he will always try his utmost to prove that he is right and she is wrong. In the second way, the moment his wife expresses the negative the man will immediately agree with her and will thereby effectively leave the decision to her. But when the man does either of these things, he inadvertently throws the woman into a state of insecurity. In the first case she becomes fearful to express her perspective, because the man invariably gets upset and angry with her. In the second case, because the woman is being forced to make all the decisions, she will soon be accused by her husband of being too bossy and of wanting to wear the pants. Both of these courses of action make the woman insecure in herself, for what is she to do? Because the male is too insecure to take any action his wife does not approve of wholeheartedly, she must either agree with everything he says, in which case she is of no real use to him, or she must just assume the male role in that relationship, in which case she will indeed be wearing the pants!

The result of this lack of intelligent co-operation between male and female is that most relationships fall into two types. The first is that type in which a very insecure male constantly dominates a wife who has no say or opinion of her own, and who to all intents and purposes is nothing more than a doormat to her husband. The second is one in which an ineffectual man behaves very much like the "little boy" with a wife who is the proverbial "mother" telling him what to do when, where and how. In the first type of relationship the male, being a very poor specimen of masculinity, is not playing his true role as the male, whilst the female has no role at all. In the second type of relationship, it is the male who has no role, whilst the woman's has become reversed, for she is now fulfilling the male role.

Although this problem is quite simple to resolve, it is not so easy in practice. Just as it takes two people to tango, so does it also take both people in a relationship to make of it a good, strong and meaningful relationship that will endure the test of time. One person alone cannot make a relationship work properly. Both the man and the woman must have knowledge of what it means to be male and female, and both of them must be willing to put that knowledge into practice, in order to achieve intelligent co-operation between the sexes. But this is where the real difficulty lies, for even when a man and a woman do have the required knowledge, the habits of a lifetime are not changed at the drop of a hat. In this respect, it is simply not possible for the male to acquire a belief in himself overnight. Neither, for that matter, is it possible for the female to acquire a trust in the male at the click of a finger. It takes time and patience, willingness and perseverance to achieve a good relationship with the opposite sex, and it takes even more effort to have a good marriage. Nevertheless, if a couple has the required knowledge, and if both are willing to work hard at it, even the most disastrous marriage can be turned into a rewarding and fulfilling experience, simply by the couple coming to acknowledge the fact that males and females think differently, and therefore that they have different perspectives on any given issue.

In addressing the deeper implications of this myth we can see that the second point, namely, that the female complements the male in every respect, really grows out of the first. If intelligent co-operation is being practised between the male and the female, then rather than the man and the woman going into competition against each other, they will instead be working together towards achieving the clarity they need. This applies both in terms of having a good relationship, as well as in being able to materialise their mutual goals.

However, here again we so often see relationships falling apart, because the male refuses to listen to his wife, or because he listens to her too much, in the sense of pushing his responsibility as the male onto her. In the first scenario either the female will do nothing to complement her husband's endeavours, out of a fear that she will upset him, or else she will become the nagging wife or the tyrannical fishwife! In the second scenario, the female definitely does nothing to complement her husband in his endeavours, for the simple reason that he doesn't have any! In this type of relationship the man is mostly only doing what his wife has decided is best for them, and therefore far from complementing her husband, she is merely using him to help her fulfil her own ambitions.

Once again the solution is simple enough, but putting it into practice is somewhat more difficult than it appears to be. The difficulty here lies in the fact that the female must learn to step back and let the male take the lead, something which is not at all easy to do when you can see that the male is dithering and doubting and not being confident in his knowledge or secure in his actions. Yet, if you wish to be a true female to the male in your life, rather than his mother, then you have no option other than to step back and to let him take the lead. In other words, you either follow the male's purpose and help him to achieve your mutual goals, or you follow your own purpose and use the male as an assistant in materialising your own goals, but you cannot do both. Once again an example may help clarify this point.

Say that you and I meet. Now my purpose in this lifetime is to reveal and disseminate the Toltec teachings, so that humanity has the necessary information with which to uplift itself, and with which to turn rotten world conditions into something more pleasant and hopeful. Now depending upon what type of person you are, you will either think I am crazy, or you will like my idea. If you like my idea, then the chances are that you and I will strike up a relationship centred around the value of the Toltec teachings, and because you believe in what I am doing you will try your best to complement my work in every way you possibly can. If that is the case, then not only will you be supporting me in my purpose, but you will also be willing to let me take the lead in the materialisation of what is now our mutual goal.

If, on the other hand, you like my idea, but are always trying to take over, in terms of wanting to tell me what to do and when to do it, the implications are that you see me as being too incompetent to bring my goal to fruition. In this case you are inadvertently undermining my belief in myself, and it will therefore not be long before I lose all confidence in myself and hand the reins over to you. Alternatively, once I have come to realise that you are, through your actions, disempowering me, I will begin to resent your bossiness, dig in my heels, and start telling you in no uncertain terms where to get off!

Should you think I am crazy, well then the chances are that you and I will just never have a relationship, let alone get married, unless of course, I really am crazy! No man wants a female in his life who thinks and tells him that he is crazy, and no woman is mad enough to marry a man she believes to be a loser! If you are wondering why I am stating the obvious here, then think again! How often do marriages not fall apart because of bad communication or, more precisely, because of the lack of intelligent co-operation? But a lack of intelligent co-operation does not imply that either of the two people are crazy.

The third point also evolves out of the previous two, because it only really comes about as a result of putting the first two into practice. When there is intelligent co-operation between male and female, and when the female is complementing the male in his purpose, the male cannot help but use both the positive and the negative to aid him in claiming his power. Power is claimed in terms of self-respect, self-confidence, and therefore also the fulfilment of both his purpose and his goal.

The concept of power is again something which goes far deeper than the scope of this little book allows for me to explain, and therefore the serious reader is advised to study this concept in greater depth by reading my first series of books. However, let it suffice for now to say that power is experiential knowledge, as opposed to information. Knowledge gained through experience is something that can be used in helping one to accomplish the task at hand or to resolve the problem one may be facing. Because it is something that can be used in a practical sense, knowledge is very much power, whereas mere information is more akin to a shot in the dark, and since it has not been tried and tested, it lacks true power.

Intellectuals like to argue that information is just as powerful as knowledge, but this is only because these people always make the mistake of placing the "power" outside of themselves. Yet true power lies within, and not without, in that true power can never be taken away or lost. A man with a gun may be termed powerful, but only for as long as he holds that gun in his hands. The moment the gun is removed from his hands, he has lost his power. Likewise, because your boss has the ability to fire you, you may well perceive him to have power over you. And indeed, for as long as you believe that your boss has that power over you, he will and does have that power! But if you work yourself into the situation where you know for a fact that you are no longer dependent upon the whims of your boss for your income, then what power will he now have over you? None!

True knowledge is knowledge of the self, and any man or woman who knows him or herself is a force to be reckoned with, for such a man or a woman has true power. For example, if you simply read the information imparted in this book, you will have gained a lot more information than you had before, but you will still be just as impotent and powerless as you were before you read it. This is because the information in itself has absolutely no power.

If, on the other hand, you use the information in this book in the sense of putting it into practice, that practice will lead to experience, and the experience will lead to knowledge of yourself and of others. Through that knowledge of yourself you can begin to change yourself in any way you wish.

To put this another way, we can say that information is very much like having a whole lot of information about writing programs for a computer, but unless you know how to operate a computer, what use is that information to you? If, on the other hand, you already know how to operate a computer, then by using that information you can write any program for any purpose you wish, and that is true power. Exactly the same is true of the human being, for unless you know what you are, and how you tick, any information you may gather will remain useless in your hands. It is a sad reflection upon humanity today that the majority of people have huge potential power, but because they have no knowledge of what makes them tick, that potential power remains firmly out of their reach. This is exactly the same as someone who does not understand computers will be at a loss as to how to make that machine work for him or her.

To return to the point under consideration, we can now see what is really implied when we talk of the female supporting the male in claiming his power. By virtue of the female simply being who and what she is, the male is able to gain a tremendous amount of knowledge about himself. To understand this, remember that we all have an inner counterpart of the opposite sex, but because none of us can interact directly with that inner counterpart we all need a physical plane mirror, or outer reflection, of that inner half of ourselves. Therefore the female is very much a mirror to the male of his own inner female, and if he acknowledges this fact then there never is any problem in practising intelligent co-operation, for the simple reason that it makes no sense to fight or to ignore a part of oneself! However, realise that by supporting the male to claim his power, the female is, of course, also using the outer male in her life to support her own inner male!

The very clear implications here are that it is only by supporting the male in her life that the female can get in touch with her own inner male, for unless she supports the outer male, she will be suppressing her inner male! Once again, it doesn't make sense to want to suppress part of oneself.

But what does this actually mean? Quite simply, it means that only by acknowledging and working with our own inner counterparts can we ever be whole, and unless we are whole, how can we ever achieve anything of real meaning in our lives?

As far as the male is concerned, he needs the negativity of the female polarity in order to achieve clarity in terms of purpose, direction and action, for without having both polarities there can never be clarity. Unless we can clearly see both the pros and the cons, both the positive as well as the negative, there can at best be only be a one-sidedness that is thoroughly subjective rather than objective.

As far as the female is concerned, exactly the same is true, except that the implications are naturally very different. Because the female needs to support her inner male, so as not to suppress a part of herself, she must also use the outer male in her life as a mirror for her inner male. Therefore it is only by also supporting the outer male that she can support her inner male, and this means that she must take the outer male's lead. Unless the woman wants to dominate her inner male, in which case she will be suppressing him, she has no other option than to hand the reins over to the outer male on the physical plane. Only in this way can she support her inner male. Doing anything else will merely plunge her headlong into the role of the mother, and in no time at all she will be threatening every man in her sight!

If you wish to threaten the men in your life, then that is fine, but then don't complain if your relationships are not working for you, and if every man resists you and fights you at every turn. If, on the other hand, you do wish to become a true female, you will also quickly come to realise that, far from being weak, the true female holds enormous power by allowing herself to take the male's lead. To grasp this, let us look at what it really entails.

Earlier it was mentioned that it is only possible to reveal the mystery of the female when she becomes incorporated into the awareness of the male. This means that the females awareness first of all has to be made part of the known, and this only comes about through the intelligent co-operation between herself and the male. Then, because the male is including her into his world, i.e. the known, her natural negativity now becomes a useful commodity and not just a threat. As a result, the female can now concentrate on being a true female, instead of having to compete against the male. Having been included in the equation of the male (the known), the female now has her own intrinsic value, and therefore rather than having to fight males to get them to acknowledge her, (in which case they never will), the male now becomes eager to listen to her and to take her guidance into full consideration. The irony here lies in the fact that if the female wants to be the male's equal, she must first be willing to step back and to take his lead. And if she does, he happily and willingly elevates her to the status of his equal!

If this sounds like male chauvinism to you, then I urge you to think very, very carefully! It is not men who made universal law. All of us are just the products of life, and we come into life as either men or women. We have a choice as to whether we like it or not. We have a choice as to whether we wish to fight universal law or make it work for us. And above all, we have a choice as to whether we wish to claim our power or dissipate it!

If men try to suppress the female, they only succeed in suppressing one polarity of their total awareness, and so they become one-sided and subjective. Lacking in objectivity, they become ever more withdrawn, which in its turn leads to a lack of inspiration and therefore creativity, and this ultimately also causes the male to become ineffectual. By suppressing his own inner female, the male disempowers himself, for instead of including the unknown within the equation, he is now working only with the known, that is, himself, or at least the little he knows of himself. Of his own inner counterpart he knows virtually nothing, and therefore how can he possibly include the unknown within the equation? Refusing to listen to the female, such a man lacks clarity, and therefore his vision too is clouded, his goal is not clear even to himself, and in having nothing but a vague goal he lacks a real sense of purpose and direction. Such a man is engaged in that infertile, unproductive activity I personally term "mental masturbation."

Similarly, if women try to dominate the male, they only succeed in materialising one half of the female awareness, namely, the mother. Of their own inner male they remain completely oblivious, and being oblivious to the true purpose and role of the male, such women have no respect for the men in their lives. This in turn also implies that they have no respect for their inner male, for a part of themselves. But it is simply not possible to respect your heart and not your liver. You either respect all of your body, or you abuse all of it. Even if you swear blind that your heart is more important than your liver, you will in practice die very quickly should you abuse your liver! Wanting to mother everything in sight, the woman who dominates the male soon enough becomes a toothless and infertile old hag! As mother, you may well be able to say "Jump!," and everyone around you may well ask "How high?", but to what effect? Is that what you want for yourself? Is that what femininity means to you? Do you see men only as little boys to do Mommy's bidding, which occasionally also means being used by Mommy as a dildo?

Women are indeed far from weak, but because the true female consciously chooses to step back in order to take the male's lead, she will often appear to be weak. However, whenever the female steps back for the male, every true male knows without any shadow of a doubt that he is ensnared even more firmly than any animal caught in a trap. Every true male can sense the implications when the female cocks her head to look up at him with such innocence. She might be smiling ever so sweetly, but in his heart of hearts he already knows that that female waiting upon his lead has chosen him to show the direction and, having been chosen, there is no escape. The male knows that one way or another she will stalk him, manipulate him, kick his butt, or do whatever else it takes to get him to claim his power as a male. When he does so, he will lead the two of them into fulfilling what she can sense is both his purpose as well as that of her own inner male. And yet, all the time she will be so sincerely encouraging, so uplifting, so supportive, but also so utterly staunch in her belief in him! What male can resist such a temptation? What kind of a male would even want to try to escape it? No! The true female may appear to be weak, but in that "weakness" lies her greatest power over the male, and indeed also over every other woman who has traded her skirts for a pair of pants!

In our treatment of this first myth we have also laid the foundations for the other eight, and therefore we will be able to cover the remaining myths rather more quickly. We will also begin to see how interrelated they all are. What will help you greatly throughout our study of the myths, is if at the end of each you make for yourself a list of all the ways in which you fail to live according to the information and principles imparted. If you do this, you will very quickly come to see the causes of your behaviour, and once that much is clear, you will be well on your way to being able to change yourself and your ways. Remember, knowledge of the self is true power!

CHAPTER SEVEN

MYTH TWO

Women are defenceless

The underlying truth of this myth lies buried in the fact that the female must be able to relate in the true sense of the word. But in order to grasp what this really means, let us first look at what is implied by the term "defenceless."

Most people have absolutely no idea what it means to be defenceless within the process of life, for in their minds there exists only the idea that "It is me and the big bad world out there, and everybody and everything is out to get me!" As a result, people tend to be highly defensive, and in the process they never come to realise that by being so defensive no-one can get near to them, not even a friend! And spouses? Well, needless to say, they are the biggest threat of all!

Confrontation is one thing, but being defensive is an altogether different kettle of fish. If someone threatens me in some way, then I have the right to confront that person should I wish to do so and, if need be, even to defend myself physically against that person. But it is not really physical defence we are talking about here, for we are in search of what it means to be a true female. As we have seen, this means that we are working with awareness, and awareness cannot be physically endangered. Therefore the type of threat we are considering here is that type which threatens our self-image, our pet theories and beliefs and, most important of all, our pet prejudices and preconceived ideas. However, if we are really wanting to gain knowledge of our true selves, why should we wish to defend such garbage! We ought to welcome confrontation by being completely de-fenceless, that is, without hurriedly wanting to erect barricades between ourselves and our opponent.

People hate having their buttons pushed, and yet the only reason why this is so, is because none of us like having our noses rubbed in our weaknesses. We prefer to pretend that those weaknesses are not there, and then whenever they cause us to stumble and fall, we either try to hide that failure, or else we become almighty cross with whoever happens to have noticed it. Does that sound familiar? But consider how utterly futile and unintelligent this behaviour really is. If you keep spilling hot tea into your spouse's lap every time you want to hand him a cup of tea, why should you become angry and upset when he points out to you that it may be better to put the cup down on the coffee-table next to him? No! If you really want to become a true female, then you should not try to defend the very stuff that is causing you to fail in your endeavours.

If we wish to master anything, be it playing a musical instrument, playing tennis, achieving a degree at university, or gaining knowledge of what it is to be a true female, we need, more than anything else, a willingness to be completely open and defenceless. In other words, we need to be totally honest with ourselves. Pretending that you play the violin beautifully when in fact you make it screech and wail, or pretending that you are an expert on the tennis court when in fact you cannot even hit a soccer ball with a bat as big as a bicycle wheel, is just plain stupid. And what's more, it is also painfully clear to everyone else that you are a fake, and stupid on top of it, for trying to pretend that you are so accomplished! Therefore by being defensive, who are you actually trying to kid? The only person you are kidding is yourself.

If you are always on the defensive and desperately try to justify every word spoken and every action committed, you are not being open – you are just being a bigot who does not know the difference between defensiveness and confrontation, that is, confrontation of the self. In being defensive the only thing you accomplish is to defend a point that you inherited from somewhere along the line, either from your social conditioning, or from a prejudice or a preconceived idea. By defending it, you are just wanting to be right, even if everyone around you can clearly see that you cannot play either the violin or tennis to save your life!

Wanting to be right has got nothing to do with the real meaning of confrontation. Confrontation means that you have the honesty necessary to confront your own behaviour openly and defencelessly whenever you notice it yourself, or whenever someone else is kind enough to point it out to you. I say "kind7 because I mean kind. Unkind people will not risk your anger by telling you the truth - instead they will giggle and laugh at your foibles behind your back. Only the kind soul who truly cares about you will also point out to you your failures.

Of course, being defenceless does not mean that you have to be a doormat. However it does mean that, as a true female, you must be open enough, defenceless enough, to be able to relate, firstly, to the male; and secondly, to the meaning of freedom. In our treatment of the first myth, we have to some extent already covered one aspect of what it means to relate to the male. The other aspects will become clear as we continue to work our way through the myths. But what about the concept of freedom? Freedom from what?

The concept of true freedom is vast, but for our present purposes it is sufficient to look only at the face value of freedom. In our heart of hearts, we would all like to be free from the debilitating restraints of our social conditioning. Because of this, freedom means having the freedom as an individual to think for yourself, and to act on your own steam, rather than always having to dance to the tune of society, and being dictated to by restrictions imposed upon us by the beliefs and prejudices of others. Freedom means having what it takes to be a female in your own right, and not to be a female like your mother, or like your grandmother, or your great-grandmother.

Naturally, freedom to live our lives according to our own standards implies that we as individuals also have our own set of values which we believe to be the right ones for us personally. If the values we hold are indeed the right values, then we should be able to see the proof of that from the results we are getting within the process of life. In other words, in relating to the male, as well as to the world around her, the female must be open enough, defenceless enough, to see for herself if what she believes in and practises is actually successful, or not. If what she is doing is working, then obviously it is a right value. But if she can see that whatever she is doing keeps causing the wheels to come off, then she must assume that either she has misunderstood what could possibly be a right value, or alternatively, the value itself could be wrong.

This whole book is about the right values within the process of life, and therefore by the time you have finished reading this, you will be in a position to decide for yourself whether you personally agree with these values or not. But for now and, as a rule of thumb, whenever you are in doubt about whether something is a right value or not, learn to look at it objectively. Whenever we are doubtful or confused about a particular issue or value, we have only to look at the same in somebody else's life, and it suddenly becomes so very easy to see whether you agree with it or not. Does that sound familiar? Yes, it should, since deep down inside we all know what is right and what is wrong. The only problem is that we do not always want to acknowledge to ourselves what we really do know. Sometimes it is just a whole lot easier to keep fooling ourselves. At other times it is such a nice escapism to pretend that we do not know, and that we are confused. In this way we can justify to ourselves, and to others, many an act which we know for a fact is neither right nor honourable.

This then brings us back to the concept of confrontation, for if you are ever going to relate to the male in your life, you must first of all be free to do so. In the final analysis, freedom means that you are open enough to be defenceless. True freedom means that you live a good, strong life based upon values you know are right. If you do that, you will have nothing to defend, no acts to justify and no buttons that anyone can push, even if everyone around you were to try their utmost to challenge you on everything in your life. To be able to stand tall and proud, and to be able to answer calmly and confidently, any question fired at you, knowing within your heart of hearts that you have nothing to hide, that you have nothing to defend and therefore that you are right, is a freedom which cannot be expressed in words. But such a freedom can only be acquired once we have made the decision to be defenceless in confronting firstly, ourselves; and secondly, others.

You will find it enormously useful if you now write down your own examples of how or when you choose to be defensive rather than to confront either yourself or others. If you do this, you will be amazed to see what utter rubbish you have come to accept as being the right values in life. You will begin to realise how the values you hold are not actually your own values, but are values which you have inherited from somewhere or someone, and which you have never really questioned. Most people's values are values learnt from their parents, from their teachers, and from what they just somehow or other picked up in their lives through social conditioning. Worse still, these values are just assumed to be right, when in actual fact they have never been questioned, nor consciously tried and tested as to their validity and effectiveness. And then on top of all of that, you will also find a whole heap of so-called values which you carry around with you, but have never actually put into practice. Why then carry all that junk? What happened to your own values? Or have you never had your own?

Strange creatures, are we not? We willingly put upon our shoulders the yoke offered to us by others, and then we wonder why our lives are such a burden! We allow others to direct our lives, and then we wonder why we constantly drive into a brick wall. Yet, because of our fear of confrontation we never actually confront ourselves or others. Instead we just keep defending values which are not our own, and rather than changing the values, we keep justifying the fact that every time we drive into a brick wall the wheels come off!

CHAPTER EIGHT

MYTH THREE

Women must be subservient

❧

This is perhaps the cruellest myth of all, since it has caused millions of women the world over, and throughout the ages, to be abused horribly, physically, emotionally and mentally, by every Tom, Dick and Harry. And yet, buried deep within its roots, is a vital truth – a truth which is so extensive in its implications that several books can be written on this one myth alone. However, for our present purposes we will keep it as brief and as compact as possible. Therefore, put quite simply, we find that the underlying truth in this myth is that women need to be contained. Let us see what this really means.

The female is by nature chaotic, for being the tonal, which is every-thing, she more often than not thinks one thing whilst feeling another. As a result, it is perfectly normal for the female to be busy with several things at the same time, whilst also being perfectly capable of finding order within disorder, and logic in the irrational. From an objective point of view it may appear that the female's life is a disorderly chaos, but within that mixture of the known and the unknown, the partially completed tasks amidst several new projects, the mixture of clear thoughts and only vaguely sensed feelings, the female knows exactly where she is and where she is going.

Therefore every female has the ability to talk to a friend on the telephone while cooking breakfast, seeing to it that Johnny brushes his teeth before going to school, reminding her husband that his great aunt is coming to dinner that evening and that he must therefore not forget that she likes her gin and bitters at six-thirty sharp, that he must not wear jeans, as his aunt detests them, and that he must remember to fetch Johnny from his soccer match on the way home. In between all of this, it is also not uncommon that the female will also rescue the parrot from its fight with the dog, remember to feed the parrot and the cat, phone Johnny's school to find out if Johnny really did not have any homework the day before, and make a mental note that on Friday evening she and her husband have to attend the birthday party of a friend who has asked her to bring special Perrier water stocked at that odd little shop just two blocks from the library off Markson Street, where parking can be found up the alleyway behind the supermarket at which she can also buy Johnny a new pair of soccer shorts, for it is so much cheaper there, and, oh yes, then she can at the same time drop off her books at the library! All that activity, planning, thinking and recollecting within the space of breakfast-time, whilst also doing her make-up, drying her hair and getting suitably dressed for a cold day that could become warmer later on whilst she is in town, where it could become difficult to find somewhere to take off her vest!

It might look like a total chaos, but for the female, this is order within disorder and logic within what, for the male, is more akin to highly irrational mental gymnastics! How on earth did she know the dog had knocked over the parrot's perch in the sewing room whilst she was talking to her friend on the telephone in the kitchen, checking Johnny's teeth and frying eggs? How does she manage to feed the parrot and the cat in the midst of drying her hair, without becoming upset and flustered? And how does she know about parking in the alleyway when he can never find parking anywhere? Perrier water? Prices? Six-thirty for gin and bitters? He could have sworn that the last time aunty came to visit she had whisky on the rocks. But then coming to think of it, maybe it was because they had run out of bitters. No jeans? Aunty doesn't approve of jeans? How did she know that, for Pete's sake? Aunty never talks about anything other than playing bridge and the fact that she disapproves of the political machinations of the right wing!

However, although this state of being is natural for the female, she can only really fulfil her role successfully if she is being contained, by a male in her life. If she is not being contained this state of being will either force her into going over the top, or else it will cause her to start feeling inadequate and somehow inferior. But what does it mean to be contained?

Being contained does not mean that the female is being suppressed or dominated in any way. Instead it means that the male has absorbed her fully into his life, in such a way that she feels acknowledged, loved and cared for. If the male does this, he automatically values her opinion and feelings with respect to all of their mutual endeavours and will always take them fully into account. By acknowledging, loving, caring for, and so, fully absorbing the female into his life, the male makes sure that the female is always included in all of his decisions and plans. Consequently, the female does not have to worry about where they are going, or whether they have enough finances for the bond on the house, or whether the insurance premiums are up to date, for she knows her male's strategy and plans as the provider, and therefore she also knows that he is seeing to all of that. Being freed in this way, she can now concern herself with the needs of the moment, irrespective of whether that means having to rescue the parrot, phone the school, organise dinner or remind her husband to fetch Johnny after soccer.

The result of this intelligent co-operation between male and female is that the female now has the freedom, not only to cope with the needs of the moment, but also to go into the unknown, and there to search her own feelings in connection with the male's quest for clarity. Knowing that she does not have to worry about hunting and providing as such, for that is the male's responsibility, the female can instead concentrate on how best to guide him in achieving the clarity he seeks. This she does, not because she is clairvoyant, but simply because she is so highly skilled in doing multiple tasks simultaneously, that she can and does sense the interrelationship of everything. In fact, it is exactly because of her ability to sense the interrelationship of all, that she is able to do so many things at once. Yet, this ability is very much a sensing rather than a knowing and so, the true female can seldom explain to the male why she feels something in a certain way. Such feelings she will simply dump in his lap, and it is then up to him to figure out what those feelings translate into, and what best to do with the facts uncovered in this way. To see how this works in practice, let us look at an example.

Say that Clint has been offered the opportunity to invest in a small printing business, and has just the evening before asked his wife, Claire, what she feels about the proposal. At first Claire does not really know what to think about this, except that she somehow feels it could be a good investment, provided Clint knew more about the practicalities involved in printing. Realising that Claire is right, in that he does not know very much about the printing business, Clint sets out the following morning to hunt down as much information as he can about printing. That same morning, Claire receives a phone call from a friend who tells her that the husband of a friend of hers has just started up a business importing paper at bargain prices. Just then Claire hears the parrot screeching from the sewing room and, sensing that his perch has been knocked over, she rushes and finds the dog and parrot engaged in a violent disagreement. Having rescued the parrot, Claire returns to the phone with the vague feeling that the incident with the parrot, the news about the imported paper and the highly indignant dog are all somehow connected to something she should be taking note of.

Later in the morning, Claire is preparing to do some shopping for dinner that night, but remembers that she must also return her library books before the end of the week. Thinking about the books and the library, Claire decides to drop the books off on her way to do the shopping and, at the same time, to see if she can find in the library any books on printing that Clint might find useful.

Claire does not end up finding anything enlightening about printing at the library, but talking to one of the librarians, the lady suggests that Clint should try to get the information he is seeking from the Chamber of Commerce and Industry. Armed with at least that much information, Claire goes shopping and then home. Once home, she phones Clint to tell him about the librarian's suggestion.

In the meantime, Clint has also been asking around for more information on the printing business, and has found out that unless the printer has access to paper at a reasonable price, it can be a risky business. When he shares this information with Claire on the phone, she excitedly tells him about the news her friend gave her that morning, and then goes on to tell him about the librarian's suggestion. But after the phone call, Claire, for some strange reason, begins to feel uneasy about something she cannot put her finger on.

Later in the day, while engaged in conversation with Clint's great aunt, Claire tells the aunt about the incident with the parrot and the dog, but the aunt, in her usual offhand manner, dismisses the incident with a wave of her hand. She sarcastically goes on to point out that dogs tend to be just as stupid as their masters, especially when, having knocked someone off his perch, they end up being far too honourable, because of a misplaced sense of loyalty, to put up a really good fight for their own rights.

Once again Claire gets that uneasy feeling that all of this is somehow connected to something she should be taking note of.

However, it is only later, when Clint joins them for drinks, and tells them about his own day, including his trip to the Chamber of Commerce and Industry, that Claire begins to see the thread of meaning in what she had been sensing all day. When he tells them that the only thing he managed to learn from the Chamber of Commerce is that there is fierce competition between printers, Claire suddenly realises that this is what the parrot and the dog had showed her that morning. So it is now clear that if Clint is going to get ahead in this business, he will, as his aunt pointed out earlier, have to be prepared to fight for his rights.

Later that evening, once Aunty has gone home, Claire shares her insight with Clint and, in absorbing what Claire noticed, Clint realises that if he is going to make a success of the printing business, he will indeed have to put aside his natural tendency not to want to impose himself upon others, in that he will not be able to afford to worry about knocking others off their perch, as it were. Clint now concludes that the only way he will be able to compete in the printing business, is to use his and Claire's newly-found contacts in the paper industry to undercut other printers, even if this means that these other printers will possibly go out of business.

Whilst both of them have been fulfilling their own roles within daily life, Clint has found the clarity he was seeking, and Claire helped him enormously in his task, even though she never once neglected her own duties, or in any way tried to assume the male role of being the hunter. From this example it should also be clear how the female can and does take the male's lead. Once

Clint had made his intention plain, Claire did not question or try to invalidate her husband's interest in the printing business, but busied herself with following the direction he had pointed out. In doing so, she also ended up giving him full support in his sense of purpose.

Rather than playing the doormat and simply agreeing with Clint that going into the printing business was an excellent idea, Claire co-operated intelligently by using her own feelings to help Clint find the necessary clarity. As a result of her actions and her input, she very much provided him with a counterbalance. Without that counterbalance, Clint may well have embarked upon the business in full trust, and without having done the necessary research first. Moreover, by having done her part, in her own inimitable female fashion, in practising intelligent co-operation, Claire also complemented the efforts of her husband fully, in every way she could. Finally, by not telling her husband what to do, when to do it and where to do it, but simply by bringing him the information he needed in order to achieve clarity, Claire did not allow herself to assume the role of mother. Instead, she chose the female route and stepped back, thus allowing Clint to make up his own mind with respect to the business. By doing this, she is also supporting him to claim his power amongst his competitors if he does decide to go ahead with the business.

We can also look at all of this in a slightly different way, by saying that the female has two options open to her. The first is to go into competition against the male and fight him. In this case he will have no respect for her, for no male can respect a second-rate male. The second is to acknowledge the fact that the male must contain her in such a way that she will take his lead, follow his direction and support his purpose, not because he is forcing her into submission and subservience, but because she believes in his sense of purpose, vision and ability.

Looked at in this light, it becomes apparent that containing the female means also winning her trust and keeping that trust, something which is only possible if the male is strong and clear, confident and creative. No female can possibly trust a man who is weak and feeble-minded. Neither can she respect such a man when he wishes to enforce his weakness upon her physically, emotionally or mentally. This is in fact no different to the way in which the government of a country contains its citizens. If the government is strong and clear, confident and creative, the people flourish and prosper, and everyone is happy, because they feel safe, secure and cared for in being contained. But if the government is weak and feeble-minded, the people begin to suffer, become restless and angry, and it is not long before crime, violence and anarchy begin to destroy peace and prosperity. In exactly the same way must the female too be contained, in the sense that she must feel secure in knowing what it is the male believes in, and what it is he is striving to achieve. Only then can she define her own role and thereby support the male in his purpose, so that they both can benefit.

In the example of Clint and Claire we can clearly see the reflection of the analogy concerning the government of a country. Just as it is the government who provides the people with the safety and security they need in order to go about their daily business in fulfilling their own purpose, so too does the male provide for the female, so that she can fulfil her purpose. Yet, the purpose of the government is also the purpose of the people, and if it is not, we have anarchy. Just as the government is chosen by the people because it has a purpose the people can believe in, so too does the female choose a male because she believes in his purpose. Therefore she will do her utmost to support that purpose, so that she can flourish and prosper in her own pursuit of fulfilment and happiness.

However, once a government has been chosen, it is senseless to fight that government, unless, of course, it turns out to be fraudulent. One must lead and one must support, for such are the universal rules of intelligent co-operation. As a friend once remarked to me, "There is no point in having a dog if you want to do the barking." Likewise is there no point in electing a government if the people wish to overrun that government.

If a government is to do its job properly, it must set about containing the efforts of the people who elected it. This it does by fulfilling its purpose, the bottom line of which is its true role. And if that government is to be successful in its role, then the people must support it, and for no other reason than the fact that the government and the people are two sides of the same coin, just as the male and the female are the two polarities of awareness. A government without a country is nothing but a useless unproductive group of people. And a male without a female is equally unproductive, remaining just an ordinary man. But a country with no government is a chaotic mess, just as a female without a male to contain and direct her will eventually succumb to chaos.

A government and the people are one, just as male and female are one, and it is this interrelationship between government and people, between male and female, that determines the interaction and interdependence termed intelligent co-operation within the process of life.

Having stated these facts, I must nevertheless also point out that none of this can be taken purely at face value. The reason for this is that male and female pertain to states of awareness, and since all of awareness is relative, it should never be forgotten that we must take into account the relative factor of awareness. Therefore a bachelor is not necessarily an unproductive and useless man. Such a man may well be the director of his own business, in which case he will very much be the male relative to all of his employees within that business, irrespective of their gender. If he is a good male, and contains his employees properly, the business will flourish, and so too will his employees. If he does not contain his employees, they will be without leadership, without direction, and therefore without any real sense of purpose, other than to grab what they can whilst the going is good. Such a business must and will fail, with the result that the employees too will suffer.

However, the above is not entirely true of a woman. The reason for this is that in order to be a true female she must support the male, her counterpart. Therefore although a woman can become the director of her own business, or even the Prime

Minister of a country, such a role denies her the possibility of realising her full potential. To be a director or, for that matter, a Prime Minister, that woman must assume the male role relative to the business or the country, and such a role will place her very firmly in the role of the mother. There is simply no other way, unless this woman has a male in her life who is containing her and leading her. However, if that is the case, then know that although such a woman may appear to be a director or a Prime Minister, she is in fact only the public figurehead, for leading her behind the scenes is her chosen male.

Although feminists will try to shout me down furiously, and will accuse me of being a male chauvinist, remember that you cannot blame me or any other male for universal laws that were not designed by men. It is true that men, in their ignorance and weakness, have abused those laws so as to suppress women and to deny them their rights, but this does nothing to change those laws. Neither men nor women can change the natural scheme of things, since this is far beyond our ability to change. We can violate these laws if we wish, but as with any violation of law, there is always a penalty attached to every violation. Thus it is not a question of me wanting to violate the rights of women – it is rather the feminists who are doing the violating, by encouraging women to assume only the role of the mother, in denial of their true femininity.

There is nothing to stop any woman from doing what she wishes to do. She can, if she chooses, become the director of her own company. She can become the Prime Minister of her country. She can be ordained as a priest and lead her congregation. She can join the armed forces and become a great military leader. In fact, apart from the sexual act, there is nothing a man can do which a woman cannot do even better. But there is one thing which neither men nor women can escape, namely, that there are consequences to every decision we make and every act we implement.

It is simply not possible to save your money and spend it. It is simply not possible to have your cake and eat it. It is simply not possible to be male and female. You either save your money, or you spend it. You either manifest your masculinity or you forfeit it. You either claim your femininity by becoming a true female, or you forfeit that birthright.

To reverse our roles as male and female, although perfectly possible, is not the answer, for the most pure and simple reason that it brings no joy and no fulfilment. You can be the most successful and powerful woman in the world, but every male in your life, no matter how strong he is, will be female relative to you unless you take his lead, follow his direction and support his purpose. Further, even with the best sex-change in the world, you will always still be only a second-rate male! I cannot change that, and neither can you, or any other woman! We do not dictate universal law. We simply make those laws work for us by co-operating intelligently with them.

If the mystery of the female is going to be resolved, then she must be incorporated into the known. This means that she must become a part of the life of the male, and support his purpose. That purpose is to incorporate the unknown into the known, that is, to solve the mystery of the female, to solve the mystery of the tonal. Why? Simply because we cannot use something which we do not know or understand, irrespective of whether we are men or women. And just as it is the male who carries the life-giving sperm, so too is it he who has to impregnate the female, so that she can bring to birth his purpose. This enables both of them to map out the unknown and to solve the mystery of the tonal, so that the female can be included within the life of the male. Without that inclusion there is nothing productive – there is only stagnation and sterility. Without that inclusion there is only the battle of the sexes or, worse·still, the reversal of the roles of the male and female.

Finally, before we leave this myth, consider why it is a man writing this book, and not a woman. If you have been wondering about this, then maybe now you can grasp why. I have little doubt that there are women out there who could have written this book better than I. But the question is, "Can you as a female take the lead of another woman?" If not, I rest my case. As a true female you will take my lead, for in your heart of hearts you know what I say rings true. Whether or not you take my lead is your choice, your decision, and finally your responsibility. I can only be held responsible for the consequences of your decision should you choose to take my lead. If not, then the consequences of your decision are not my responsibility.

CHAPTER NINE

MYTH FOUR
Women don't think

In considering this perfectly silly old myth we will see how in effect we are still only adding in the details pertaining to Myth One. But what truth is hidden within this myth? The truth we are seeking is that it is wrong for the female to rationalise, for if she does, she cannot possibly support the purpose of the male. In order to grasp this let us look more closely at what it means to rationalise.

To rationalise, basically means that we can make excuses for anything, and we can make ourselves believe anything that we want to. To rationalise is quite literally what the word tells us, namely, that you consider the options open to you within any given issue, and you come to a decision as a result of having weighed up your options. However, rationalisation does not necessarily mean that what you have come up with is right. In fact, most of the time it is just a question of choosing the lesser of two evils, and just because something is the lesser of the two evils it does not make that evil right. Deep down inside we all know what are the right values in life, and no matter how hard we try to rationalise wrong action, we cannot ever justify the fact that we know we are doing something which we can feel, or sense, is wrong.

Not to rationalise does not mean that you must not use your mind, but it does mean that you must take care as to how you use your mind. In using your mind you must remember that your life, your purpose and your fate is completely tied in with that of the male. Therefore, in order to be a true female you must learn to direct your thinking in terms of how best you can aid the male, firstly, to achieve his purpose, and secondly, to fulfil his fate.

It may help if we digress at this point to clarify what is meant by fate versus purpose. Fate is not really what people have come to believe it is. Fate is the mission, or the task, assigned to us in this incarnation. However, since very few people ever really know what it is they are meant to be doing in this lifetime, they can only really be guided towards the fulfilment of their fate through the medium of feeling. Being alert to, and then following our feelings translates into a sense of purpose. Feeling, in this sense, is very much what is described as gut feel or intuition, and when it is strong, that is, not being suppressed by rationalisation, it can and does guide people into achieving phenomenal success in their lives. Such success is not confined only to financial success, but also includes success in relationships, in achieving happiness and satisfaction and, in short, in fulfilling one's fate. Therefore fate is the mission we have to accomplish in this lifetime, and purpose, or more precisely, the sense of purpose, is what guides us into how best to fulfil that fate.

If we return now to what we are considering, namely, that in order to be a true female you must learn to think in terms of how best you can aid the male, firstly, to achieve his purpose, and secondly, to fulfil his fate, we can see that what this boils down to is that you are quite frankly manipulating the male. By aiding the male in this way you are urging him into getting on with the job, so that you too can achieve your purpose and fulfil your fate which, remember, also happens to be his fate. The fact that your chosen male will have the same fate as you, should not be surprising, if you recall that the only reason you chose this particular male is because you believe in his purpose. But to believe in a purpose means that it is also your purpose, reflecting your fate. It is impossible to believe in a purpose which is contrary to one's fate, although, admittedly, some misguided people do try to force themselves into such odd behaviour.

Having clarified this point, we now come to the million dollar question, namely, "How to achieve this?" The best way in which to do this, as we saw in the example of Claire in the previous chapter, is to follow your female intuition, or your gut feel. What this really means is that we must learn to listen to our hearts.

Everyone has been taught, or rather, encouraged, to ratio-nalise, but none of us have ever been taught to listen to our hearts. Listening to the heart means listening to our gut feel, and then acting upon those feelings, rather than acting upon rational assumption. The rational mind is in fact only the human being's own in-built computer and, just like any computer, is only as good as the information stored in it. But the information stored in the computer, in the rational mind, is what constitutes one's view of the world. That view of the world is based mostly upon preconceived ideas and prejudices, and is therefore quite literal-ly the way in which we have become conditioned into looking at everything in our lives, including what it is to be female. Furthermore, because people have become conditioned into living in their heads, instead of listening to their hearts, that con-ditioning, which is a part of their view of the world, has also bred in people the desire to rationalise, in their attempts to justify wrong action. As a result, few people really listen to their hearts – instead they engage in endless internal chatter that goes round and round in the mind indefinitely. But clearly, that internal chatter has got nothing to do with listening to your heart.

As paradoxical as it may appear at first, listening to the heart is in fact true thinking. The academics of this world do not like to admit it, but the truth of the matter is that all so-called "great minds" act upon feeling. Therefore, irrespective of whether it is a new invention, a remarkable discovery in science, a musical composition or a great work of art, the creativity that has led to such works has its origin in feeling. Only once that feeling has been translated into a mental vision of what can be, does the inventor, scientist, composer, or artist use the rational mind to work out the practicalities involved in materialising his vision.

In trying to listen to our hearts it is vitally important that we remember always to look upon our life as one whole, that has both meaning and purpose. If we do not do this, then our life always appears to be a mixed bag of unrelated mishaps and luck which seem to make no real sense at all. If we see our life in terms of a mixed bag of odds and sods, then it is clear that we cannot possibly glean any real sense of purpose, let alone gain a vision of our fate. It is therefore necessary for us to take stock of all of our life's experience. In doing so, we must strive to be open enough, to be defence-less enough, in order to detect the connecting threads that run throughout our life. These threads not only show clearly what is really taking place in our lives, but they also inspire in us the sense of purpose that will ultimately lead us into fulfilling our fate. Besides these threads, we are always surrounded by more than enough guidance from the world around us. Therefore, all we have to do in following the threads, is to listen to this guidance, by not allowing our view of the world to close us off from what we can sense is our purpose and our fate.

It may help to show what is meant by listening to the heart if we look at a simple example. Say you have a problem in your marriage. Now you can either engage in endless internal chatter about what is wrong, about what you should do, about what you would like to do, and about all sorts of fears, doubts and worries, or alternatively, you can simply open yourself up to receiving guidance from the world around you. If you follow this latter course, you will find yourself looking at other people's marriages. This will lead you into some measure of objectivity, and in that objectivity you will soon come to see exactly where the wheels are coming off. This is what is meant by being surrounded by guidance. If you now remain open to that guidance, and you look for clarity, by distancing yourself from your internal chatter, you will also quickly enough begin to see what constitutes the real problem in your own marriage. It is quite as simple as that, but the reason why it always appears to be so very difficult and confusing is that people always allow their own preconceived ideas to clutter their minds, instead of just being completely open and honest with themselves.

Naturally, these preconceived ideas can be positive or negative. Yet a preconceived idea is still a preconceived idea, and therefore undesirable. For example, if you are not being totally open and defenceless in looking at your marriage, you may end up by positively defending your own behaviour, or even the behaviour of your husband. Yet, either way, by becoming defensive, you will once again start to rationalise, in an attempt to justify your preconceived ideas of what is happening in your marriage. The result of this is that you will serve neither your husband nor yourself. Therefore, although you may think that you are taking a positive approach in trying to keep your marriage from falling apart, if you are becoming defensive you are not being open and honest, and the marriage will still fail, if not today, then tomorrow.

On the other hand, it could be that your marriage has got to the point where you are seeing everything from a purely negative perspective. For example, if your husband has thought about you for a change, and arrives home with a bunch of roses for you, you could find yourself becoming very suspicious of him. "Why does he have to waste money like this?" "Why is he sucking up all of a sudden?" But once again, you will not be open and honest if you submit to your negative preconceived ideas, for you will be giving way to rationalisation rather than listening to your feelings and using the guidance received.

There are two important points that we always need to bear in mind. The first is that deep down inside, if only we pay attention to it, all of us can always feel what is right and what is wrong, what is working and what is not. The second is that all of us have more than enough guidance from the world around us to enable us to overcome any challenges in our lives, but in order to use that guidance we must have the openness and honesty which constitutes true defencelessness. If we remember these two points, there will never be a need or an excuse for us to rationalise – instead we will find ourselves thinking clearly, and acting with true impeccability.

CHAPTER TEN

MYTH FIVE

Women do not smoke or drink

The real meaning behind this myth is rather obscure, in that it refers to the fact that it is the male who must show through example that life, far from being a sin, is a priceless gift, because it is our only opportunity to learn. To understand this we need to look at the meaning of what people perceive as sin.

The concept of sin is a perfect example of the kind of junk that can arise out of either our own view of the world, or someone else's. We have all been conditioned into thinking that in order to be good people we must deny ourselves all sorts of things, and that to partake in the goodnesses and the richnesses of life is somehow a sin. Even those people who are not particularly religious, and who may therefore not use words such as "sin," still fall prey to humanity's concept of people being either good or evil. As a result, everyone tries their level best to con-form to what makes them "good" in the eyes of their fellow men.

However, in a world that is going mad this no longer makes any sense. Today, in order to conform to the norm, even people who in the past may have been termed good because of the values they upheld, have to abandon those good values for val-ues that are truly questionable.

For example, teenagers nowadays have to smoke, drink alcohol, use drugs, and hump away like so many sex-maniacs in order to be accepted as normal! In the past such behaviour would have been frowned upon as being sinful, but today sinful behaviour is the "in-thing!" Therefore what are we talking about? Clearly it cannot be sin, because if sin is out one day and in the next, then what is all this business about having to conform? Conform to what? Or is it just fashion that shapes our lives and sets our values?

I don't know about you, but I choose to set my own standards and define my own values in life. If someone else thinks being an alcoholic is "cool," and believes that to waste away his brain with drugs is being "sharp," well that is his opinion, but I sure as hell will not conform to his standards of self-destruction. For me, life is a truly priceless opportunity to manifest one's full potential and awareness within the world. Whilst others want to be social dropouts and become junkies, I want to get to the very top! Therefore as far as I am concerned, if some choose to drop out of society because of having become junkies, that is great, because then I have less competition! Does that sound terrible and self-centred? Good! I mean to make exactly that point, because why should I, or anyone, have to conform to someone else's cotton-wool thinking and perverted beliefs?

If there is any sin at all, then it surely must be the sin of social conditioning. There can be no greater evil than to force others into your way of thinking, so that you can impose your will upon them. Yet, this is exactly what people do, and the way this is achieved, is to manipulate others into the fear of being ostracised unless they conform! I am sure you know what I mean. "Unless you have sex with me, I will leave you." "Unless you also pump heroine, we will not accept you into our circle of friends." "Unless you lie like us, and steal like us, we will set your home on fire." And so the manipulation or, more precisely, the intimidation goes on and on, and more and more people succumb to it because of their fear.

Yet, at the bottom of this diabolical conditioning lies a great truth, namely, that there is only one life. This is undeniably true, and consequently none of us are islands existing within a vacuum. But somehow, people have come to believe that to be ostracised is to be prohibited from being able to participate fully within that wholeness we term the process of life. It is therefore not so strange that, deep down inside, people have such a huge irrational fear of being ostracised. However, that fear, and especially how it is manifesting in the world today, is purely an illusion.

In practice we can never really be ostracised in the true sense of the word. We can be kicked out by our family, we can be excluded from our circle of friends, we can be excommunicated by the church, or we can be removed from society and people in some other way, but we can never be cut off from life, for what has any of this got to do with life? Life is what we make of it through our interaction with it. So even if your friends shun you, you are still interacting with them, albeit differently to when they accepted you, but life is what you choose to do with that interaction. It is not the interaction that is life. Life is whatever you make it because of how you choose to perceive that interaction. Therefore you can choose to see yourself as being one of them. You can choose to see yourself as having been ostracised. You can choose to see yourself as a victim. You can choose to feel hurt, rejected, elated, happy, peaceful, or whatever else you may feel. But it boils down to a choice – a choice that makes it quite clear that we ourselves can, and do, decide where we wish to place the focus.

The only person who can cut you off from life is you yourself. Only you can decide to stop "living," to become morose and unhappy should your friends exclude you, or should your family disinherit you, or should the church excommunicate you. But have you ever considered that maybe they are doing you a favour? Have you ever considered that the whole reason why people would want to exclude you is because you are different to them, and therefore have different values? But only you can decide whether you like yourself and your values. Through challenging you these other people have done you the favour of forcing you to do that self-assessment. If you don't like yourself and think your values stink, then listen to these people and change yourself and your values. But if you like yourself and believe your values are good, then allow those people to get lost, for you will not be needing their company any longer! There is no need for you to become a jerk so as to keep company with jerks! Either way, the people who forced you into making the required self-assessment have done you a huge favour, so there is absolutely no need to be so upset or tearful. Be happy, for either way you win!

Being able to stand on our own feet and making our own decisions, based upon our own values, brings tremendous freedom – a freedom that also allows us to participate openly and freely of the richnesses of life. By richnesses I am not only referring to the positive, but also to the negative. If we did not have day and night, we would never know the true nature of light, and if we did not have happiness and unhappiness we would never know the true depth of happiness. We have to experience all aspects of life upon the physical plane if we are to grasp the real significance of life. This does not mean that you must be murdered in order to know the meaning of life, or that you must become a drug addict in order to know what it is to be free from drugs, but it does mean that we cannot have gaps in our knowledge. So, if you have never had a brush with death, or have never been in contact with drugs in some way, your frame of reference is limited in those areas, and therefore so too will be your understanding of life and of drugs.

I am by no means advocating that anyone should use this as a justification for wrong behaviour. If you already know that drugs are not for you, then there is no need to take drugs, and if you already know that you do not want to be a prostitute, then there is no reason to behave like one! What I am referring to, is the fact that there is no reason why we should not decide for ourselves to explore something to which we may feel attracted but which is as yet beyond our present frame of reference. In order to clarify this point, let us look at some examples.

There are a great many heterosexual men and women in this world who have, at some stage in their lives, had homosexual experiences in their journey of discovering the meaning of sexuality. But, even if these people enjoyed them, such experiences do not make them homosexual. On the contrary, such men and women normally end up being far more secure in their sexuality than they were before. To grasp this, realise that these people would not have exposed themselves to this type of experience had they been secure in their sexuality in the first place. But now, as a result of their homosexual experiences, they know beyond any shadow of a doubt that they are truly heterosexual.

Similarly, there are today many people who have at some time in their lives experimented with drugs, and who may at the time even have believed that it was enjoyable. But having had that experience, rather than spending the rest of their lives fantasising about "tripping out," they have come to the realisation that drugs and "tripping out" are not for them in the long run. Yet such experience does not make these people drug addicts.

In the same vein there are also many people who may have smoked but who now no longer smoke, or who have made a habit of imbibing too much alcohol, but who now enjoy alcohol in moderation only. There are also many people who have been seriously ill at some stage in their lives, but who are now well and healthy. So, this is the point I want to make: whenever we have an imbalance of sorts, irrespective of whether it is a physical imbalance, an emotional imbalance or a mental imbalance, we invariably manifest some sort of dis-ease. Dis-ease means that we are not at ease with our physical body, our emotions or our mind, but in all these cases it is a lack of knowledge in some area of our lives that is bringing about that imbalance and the consequent dis-ease. In time that dis-ease can become so intense that it begins to cause undue stress upon our being. If the dis-ease is physical we can become physically ill, unless we strive to alleviate the stress. Exactly the same is true of our emotional and mental states of being, if we do not strive to alleviate the build-up of emotional or mental stress that results from emotional or mental dis-ease. It is for this reason that people will often resort to smoking, alcohol or drugs, in the same way that someone suffering from physical dis-ease will resort to the use of medication.

Dis-ease does not necessarily mean that a person is ill, but unless the cause of that dis-ease is eradicated, some form of illness will be the end result. But, as we have already noted, all dis-ease is the result of imbalance, and any imbalance is caused by a lack of knowledge. However, since all true knowledge can only be gained through experience, imbalances can only be corrected through the judicious acquisition of experience in that particular area of our lives in which we lack the required knowledge. I say "judicious," because just as medication should be administered judiciously, so too must we in these cases be prudent in our acquisition of the knowledge we lack. Just as an overdose of painkillers can kill the patient, so too can an over-indulgence in alcohol lead to alcoholism. Likewise, although many men and women have cured themselves of insecurity regarding their sexuality by allowing themselves homosexual experiences, many others still have succumbed to homosexuality, because they abandoned themselves to the experience, rather than having been judicious. Remember that we are here referring to the correction of an imbalance, and not to the normal acquisition of knowledge. In normal life we can never have too much knowledge, but in correcting an imbalance it is perfectly possible to overdose oneself.

Having gained this perspective on the importance, and the role, of knowledge in our lives, we are in a better position to grasp why, at the beginning of this chapter, I stated that it is the male who must show through example that life is not a sin. Why the male? Why sin? These are two questions which are not at all easy to answer in just a few sentences. Therefore let us consider each of them in some depth.

As we have already seen, in order to manifest our full potential upon the physical plane we cannot afford to have gaps in our knowledge, for not only will those gaps act as handicaps, but they will also cause in us an imbalance of sorts. Obviously, if we are handicapped and imbalanced we are not going to be able to fulfil our full potential. The implications here are that it is therefore necessary for us to partake fully in all of the richnesses of life, but without indulging in them. In other words, we must partake whilst at the same time standing detached.

Standing detached means coming to the realisation that although we are fully entitled to enjoy ourselves upon the physical plane, we will nonetheless get nowhere if we allow ourselves to become enmeshed by materialism. In this respect realise that it is not the physical plane as such that is important, but the knowledge we gain from life upon the physical plane. This is a subtle difference which most people tend to overlook all too often. Furthermore, it also requires considerable skill in execution, and this demands a great deal of discipline, that is, self-discipline.

However, by now it should be clear that self-discipline does not mean denial. Although most people tend to think that denial means discipline, denial is in actual fact nothing more than a form of self-punishment, and self-punishment can never help us to acquire the knowledge we seek in order to fulfil our full potential. The real meaning of self-discipline means exactly what the word tells us, namely, to be a disciple to the self. But here we should take very great care, because unless we know who our true self is, we could very easily end up becoming a disciple to our social conditioning or, worse still, becoming a disciple to our preconceived ideas or our prejudices.

From everything we have learned in our study of the myths so far, it should not be too difficult to see that the real meaning of self-discipline is that we are willing to partake in all of our life's experiences with total honesty and sincerity. If we do this, then we can also always perceive the folly and the danger of indulgence, since whenever we do indulge, we can now very clearly see how this implies that we have no self-respect. For example, if you eat in excess of what you need to satisfy your hunger, you will not only become a glutton, but you will also more than likely become overweight. But people who are gluttons and are overweight, simply do not care, because of their lack of self-respect. Therefore the important point to keep in mind in considering self-discipline, is treating oneself with respect, for it is not eating that is bad, but our indulgence in over-eating.

Equally, it is not life that is bad, and neither are our experiences in life bad. What makes our experiences good or bad is what we do with them, and what makes our lives wholesome or debauched, is our detachment or our indulgence respectively. So, we are all entitled to enjoy our lives and our experiences, provided we keep the necessary detachment to maintain self-discipline, so as to retain our self-respect. In fact, it is only by enjoying our lives to the full that we can bring out our full potential and thereby truly fulfil our fate.

However, as we know only too well, thanks to social conditioning, this tenet is very much taken at face value by most people, especially men, with the result that they will often indulge in a life of utter debauchery that lacks all trace of self-discipline and self-respect. But since it is the male who must take the lead, what sort of a lead is this? What self-respecting female can possibly take the lead from a man who is obese, an alcoholic, a drug addict or a sex maniac? Neither, for that matter, can the true female take the lead from a man who is not sure whether he should be Arthur or Martha.

Yet, sadly, there are today so many women who have cast aside both self-discipline and their self-respect through having taken the lead of men who are not true males, but petulant little boys indulging in everything their mothers would never have approved of. Therefore the real meaning of this ancient myth is that women must not emulate men, for if they do, they fall prey to a dis-ease which should be peculiar to men only. That dis-ease is the struggle which every man has in learning what it is to be a true male, rather than a petulant little boy rebelling against mother. If a woman tries to take the lead of a little boy, she will only succeed in becoming a second-rate little boy and, in the process, will lose her self-respect.

This brings us round to the concept of sin. If there is any thing that is a sin, then it is the sin against self. To abandon our quest for knowledge and to cast aside self-discipline, in order to waste away our lives in a state of disrespect for self, is possibly the only real sin there can be. It is not our experiences in life that constitute sin. It is what we do with those experiences. If we use our experiences in order to uplift ourselves and to fulfil our fate, how can those experiences possibly be bad or sinful? But if we use our experiences in life so as to lead us ever further into a lack of self-respect, then we are destroying not only ourselves, but also the truly stupendous gift of life. To destroy is not life-supporting, and to waste is a truly ungracious act of disrespect that leads to destruction.

The true male, that is, the man who has overcome the imbalance that is causing him to be a little boy rebelling against mother, will never give a lead that culminates in the destruction of self-discipline and self-respect. Because the true male has enough self-discipline and self-respect, he will also not provide a lead that culminates in a path of denial. Instead, the true male will always set the example of how life upon the physical plane can be enjoyed fully. This he does by allowing himself to partake in all of the many richnesses life offers him, but without ever losing his sense of detachment and so becoming prone to indulgence. In this way, the true male takes the lead in pointing out that in order for us to realise our full potential we cannot have gaps in our knowledge, and that if we do have an imbalance of sorts, that imbalance can be rectified without having to become "ill." But if we look at the world today, we see a great many "sick" people living in a society that is becoming evermore "sick." Why? Because men have succumbed to their dis-ease with mother, and in trying to take the lead of these little boys, women are emulating them more and more. And so sounds the refrain of Annie, "Anything You Can Do I Can Do Better!" Today it is no longer the men who brag about how much they can drink, for many women can outdrink most of them. Neither is it men who today brag about their sexual prowess, because, generally speaking, whilst most men need a while to recover after they have spent themselves, there are increasing numbers of women who are not shy of having sex with multiple partners one after the other.

CHAPTER ELEVEN

MYTH SIX

Women are gentle

T he real meaning of this myth is easier to understand, especially when we see that the truth it contains is that women must and do nurture – something which comes very naturally for any woman. In relation to this, remember that the sole purpose of life upon the physical plane is to materialise our full potential within physical life. In order for us to do this, we must all nurture the purpose of the male, and therefore the purpose of the spirit of man, irrespective of our gender.

Because the male represents the known, and the female represents the unknown, when we refer to the purpose of the male, we are implying also the purpose of the female. The reason for this is that just as it is the purpose of the male to incorporate the unknown into the known, so too is it the female's purpose to become incorporated into the world of the male. This, after all, is what is implied when it is stated that the woman complements the male.

However, the only way in which any of us, again, irrespective of gender, can support the purpose of the male, is to dream. But, since we all know that unfulfilled dreams are more than useless, we need to learn to dream in terms of a definite purpose. The reason for this is that all true knowledge can only arise out of practical experience. So, when we refer to dreaming, it is not airy-fairy thinking that is called for, but the dreaming in of action. But even with action, it is wise to bear in mind that action that does not go anywhere, or that does not yield some sort of dividend, is not only a waste of time, but also futile.

This is something which every woman is very aware of. This inner knowing comes about because, deep down inside, she can sense that the dividends she is looking for are those which result from the male having claimed his power. Consequently, all of the true female's actions are geared towards supporting the male in ways that will enable him to claim his power. Those actions automatically also include her dreaming, for all females dream of being swept off their feet by a handsome knight in shining armour atop his white stallion. Yet, encapsulated within that dream of dreams, is a deep secret of the female.

People may wish to argue this point, but there is nothing upon this earth that is more powerful than belief. The Wright brothers put aeroplanes into the sky because they believed it possible. Man has journeyed into outer space because he believed it possible. People have performed all sorts of miracles because they believed them to be possible. And a man who has a female that insists upon seeing him as a shining knight, has no option other than to live up to that belief, unless, of course, he is a total jerk wanting to take advantage of that vision so as to rape her!

Therefore when the true female dreams, she is dreaming into existence her vision of the perfect male and, in doing so, is surreptitiously but most powerfully, manipulating him into materialising that vision. Yet, if the woman is a true female, she will not want to mother the male in her practice of dreaming, but will tailor her dreaming to the purpose of the male. Instead of imposing her will upon him, and thereby violating his fate, she will dream into existence a shining knight dedicated to his own quest, his own purpose, his own fate, and she sees herself as being fated to be swept up into the arms of that man.

However, this is exactly where it is so very important to use the mind in order to discriminate with wisdom, for the female must take care that she nurtures the male, instead of mothering him, and also that in nurturing him she nurtures his strengths but not his weaknesses, for otherwise he will never claim his power as a male. The true purpose of the mind is to discriminate, that is, to work out what are the right values in life. Therefore the true female uses her mind to work out what she feels is the male's purpose, and how best she can assist him in fulfilling that purpose. Of course, we are talking here about the true female who dreams of having a real male in her life. Those women who believe that men are nothing but little male dolls, will not want to support the male's purpose, but will instead want to mother their little darling dolls and to impose upon them their own sense of purpose.

This leads us to another important concept, which is that the female needs to stand back if she is going to support the male's purpose. Standing back does not mean that the female is denied her individuality, or her independence, but it does mean that if she is going to support the male's purpose, she must take his purpose as her own. For example, although a wife is perfectly entitled to have a career of her own, she must nonetheless regard her husband's career as being more important than her own. If she does not do this, her own career will become more important than that of her husband, and eventually more important than even her husband, in which case she will be pursuing her own purpose, rather than supporting her husband's purpose. We see this all too often when, once a married couple has started a family, the female becomes so engrossed in being the mother of their children, that she not only forgets she has a husband whose purpose she once supported, but now even starts to mother him into how a father should behave!

I cannot stress enough how very important it is that the female learns to step back for the male. Although it may appear as if the female is making herself less than the male by stepping back for him, she is in effect doing nothing of the sort. In fact, the reverse is true. By making his purpose supreme, and by putting his vision first, the female is making it clear to the male that she believes in him, and trusts that he is not going to abuse her, or disappoint her in some way. By believing in the male in this way, the female in effect manipulates him, firstly, into claiming his power as a male; and secondly, into bringing forth the true female in her, rather than the mother.

It is only through the female refusing to mother the male, and by standing back, that the male can and does claim his power. Having claimed his power, he will automatically elevate the female to the status of his equal, by ceasing to rebel against her as if she were his mother. But, even more important than this, is that once the male sees the female as his partner, and not as his mother, he unconsciously begins to do everything in his power not to disappoint her in her vision of him. We can look upon this as seeking approval if we wish, yet it is not really seeking approval, but the very essence of intelligent co-operation. To grasp this, think of it in this way: "If you are willing to acknowledge me as a male, I will do my level best to prove to you I am worthy of that trust. But if you wish to mother me, I will fight you every step of the way by digging in my heels and rebelling. In this way I can at the very least prove to you, and myself, that I am not weak, and do not need your constant nagging!"

Notwithstanding any of the above, remember that the mother is a part of the female, and so cannot be bad. She also has her role to play. The art of the true female lies in her ability to judge when it is appropriate to be the mother, and when to be purely female. Here again it is most important for the female to use her mind to discriminate wisely. For example, if a man has forgotten that he is meant to set the example, and gets himself "motherless" in a bar with his buddies, then he most certainly needs mother to take him in hand. No man has ever suffered damage to his masculinity because he received a tongue-lashing from his wife, or because he was locked out of the house when he knows he behaved like a little brat. On the contrary, a hard smack through the face has brought many a man back to his senses, and being told that unless he grows up and gets his act together he can pack his bags, has made many a man angry enough to grow up instantly, and immediately to set out proving that he is indeed very much a male!

In connection with the above it is also worthwhile pointing out that the true female does not fall apart when she gets an angry response from the male in her life. Such anger from the male is inevitable whenever she is forced to play the role of mother. No man likes having it pointed out that he is a weak slob. Yet sometimes it is necessary to do just that, so that he can see it for himself and start changing his behaviour. But here it is wise for the female to remember that just as she is not really offended by the anger of her children, and does not fall apart if a reprimanded child tells her he hates her, so too is there no need for her to become highly emotional and upset when she has angered the male in her life and he starts to react like a child. No doubt, just like any little boy, he will rant and rave, or sulk, but after a while he will have to acknowledge that "mother" is right and that he is behaving like a twit!

Yet, it is still so very important for the female to treat the male like an adult, and not like a little boy. Even if it is necessary to mother the male for whatever reason, it should never be forgotten that he is an adult. Not to treat him like an adult will only bring out the very worst in the male, and it is then that such a man will tend to become physically violent and utterly abusive. Any self-respecting man will endure a physical slap through the face when he knows he has deserved it, but if he is slapped through the face like a little boy, either literally or figuratively, he is likely to explode.

As an integral part of nurturing, the female supports the male in his purpose and, in addition, involves herself in his life fully. If this involvement is lacking, it can have severe consequences. So often women cannot understand why their husbands come home from work, give them a peck on the cheek, and then spend the rest of the evening behind their newspapers, or become engrossed in some television program. But what such women have failed to appreciate, is that there is nothing worse for the male than not being able to share. Just as he is the hunter who enjoys to share the food he has brought home, and just as he enjoys to share the life-giving sperm from his loins, so too does he enjoy sharing his triumphs and his failures, his hopes and his fears, his joy and his sorrow. For the male, because he is the provider, to give is to live. But if he is made to sit down and receive all the time, he begins to feel inadequate, insecure and, ultimately, a failure. To see the effects of this, let us look at a typical example.

Gary has had a very busy day at work, and although he landed his company a most promising new contract, the negotiations for that contract were extremely difficult and trying, often coming close to a complete breakdown. Tired, but happy, Gary was looking forward to going home, pouring himself and his wife a drink, and sharing with her the experiences of his day. But when he arrives home, Gary finds his wife, Samantha, talking to a friend in the kitchen. Hardly sparing the time to kiss him hello, Samantha excitedly blurts out that her friend just got engaged the day before, and that she, Samantha, has decided that Joan should stay for supper and share all of her good news with them!

Not wanting to upset his wife, Gary agrees that it sounds like a good idea, but deep down inside, he already feels resentment. Going for a shower before changing for the evening, Gary starts to feel guilty for being selfish and petty, and so he forces himself to behave like he knows Samantha would like him to behave, not only towards her, but also towards Joan. The evening goes well, but never once during the course of the conversation is Gary given the opportunity to share his own day, for every time he tried, Samantha would say, "Not now, my love! Let's not spoil Joan's evening talking about work!" Even later that evening, after Joan had left to go home, Gary could still not share with Samantha, for all his wife could talk about was the coming wedding, what she was intending to wear, where the reception would be held, and speculating who the guests would be.

That night, after Samantha has finally cuddled up next to him in bed, yawned and fallen asleep, Gary lies awake for a long time. Alone at last, but now having to recapitulate the day's events by himself, Gary rolls to the side of the bed, as far away from Samantha as he can get. Feeling angry, but also guilty for being angry, feeling sorry for himself, but also ashamed that he should be so petty, Gary tosses and turns for a long time before finally falling asleep in a state of frustration.

The following morning, Samantha can sense that Gary is being standoffish, but she is much too busy getting ready for work herself to take much notice. Doing her make-up, she once again starts to talk about Joan's forthcoming marriage. But when Gary suddenly storms out of the house without saying goodbye, and slams the front door behind him, Samantha is utterly surprised. Left wondering what has got into her husband's head now, she mutters, "I will never understand men," and continues doing her make-up, once again busy with what dress she will wear to Joan's wedding, and what suit Gary should wear to match her dress!

That afternoon, when Gary phones Samantha at work to tell her that he will be going out with some of the office staff for drinks after work, Samantha encourages him to stay out for as long as he would like, for then she and Joan can spend the evening together planning the guest list for the wedding. By this time Gary has succumbed to his frustration, and when he finds that the bright-eyed girl who joined his company a month ago is still single and joining them for drinks after work, he starts to forget his frustration as he starts to dream. Later that evening, he discovers that the new girl has a warm smile for him, and is also very interested in hearing about his recent victory at work. When much later that night Gary comes home in a highly spirited mood, Samantha is relieved to see that her husband is once again his usual charming self, but wonders why he is not keen to make love to her.

I think the example above is self-explanatory, and it is unnecessary to spell out what will be the end result in that relationship. Unless Gary puts his foot down and claims his power as a male, he will not be able to contain Samantha, in which case she will continue to mother him until he cannot stomach it any more. Similarly, Samantha herself must begin to see what she is doing, in order to step back, stop mothering Gary, and allow him to take the lead. Ideally, in situations such as these, both people concerned should be adult enough, and open and honest enough, both with themselves, as well as with each other, to realise that they do have a problem that needs to be discussed and sorted out between themselves before it is too late.

Remember that the female must of her own accord choose to make herself a part of the male's life – he cannot force her to do so, unless he violates her freedom and her individuality. The male can provide the lead, but it is for the female to take that lead. The male can initiate the action, but it is up to the female to complement that action. Likewise the male can provide the life-giving sperm, but it is the female who has to accept it, conceive, and bring to birth that seed. If she doesn't, she in effect aborts the initiations of the male, irrespective of whether it is his physical seed, his emotional input, or his mental stimulation. If she continues to abort his initiative, and continuously tries to mother him, rather than support and nurture his purpose, the male will soon enough begin to loose heart. Having lost heart, he will seek to escape in one way or another. Either he will escape into his newspaper, or the television, or else he will escape by starting to have an affair outside of his marriage.

CHAPTER TWELVE

MYTH SEVEN
Women should not work

In order to get to the bottom of this myth it is important to understand that the woman on her own can never be truly female. As prejudiced as this may appear to be, realise that we either choose to work together with the male, or we choose to go into competition against the male. But if a woman goes into competition against the male, she only succeeds in bringing out the mother in herself, and she becomes a second-rate male.

In a great many ways this myth is really just another facet of the previous one, except that the implications here are somewhat different, in that not only must the female nurture the purpose of the male, but she must also not compete against the male. Each of them has their own role to play, and each role is equally important. Therefore, just as the male is the hunter and the provider, so is it the female who tends to the home, the hearth and brings to birth, not only the children of their marriage, but also the fruits of their mutual endeavours.

This does not mean that the woman is not allowed to have a career of her own. Nor does it mean that she must stay at home, barefoot in the kitchen and be constantly pregnant. But it does mean that whatever she chooses to do must not clash with the purpose of the male. As we have already seen, if the woman is to be a true female, then it is imperative that she steps back and allows the male to take the lead, for if she doesn't, she will end up wearing the pants.

By usurping the power of the male, the female cannot help but become a second-rate male, and this fact remains true even if the woman becomes the Premier of her country. The secret in dealing with all this lies in the female's ability to nurture, for in doing this, she nurtures the purpose of the male, and also secretly furthers her own sense of purpose.

As a result of upholding the purpose of the male, the female can and does feel very good about herself in the sense of being a true female. Because she now feels good about herself, she has uplifted both herself, as well as the male, for he will always respond to her femininity by becoming much more male himself. Being much more of a male than before, the male also feels good about himself, and in turn uplifts the female again, and so the cycle of mutual upliftment continues. Therefore instead of blaming each other, shouting and screaming at each other and, generally speaking, breaking each other down, the male and the female now have a very good process of intelligent co-operation going on between them.

The important point to notice in respect of this, is that it is the female who goes first. This means that she first of all has to step back and support the male before she can feel like a true female, and before he can respond to her like a true male.

It can, of course, also work the other way, in which case we have the well-known story of "the Taming of the Shrew." But even here, unless the female finally relents and allows herself to take the male's lead, the shrew will never be tamed, and the male will eventually give up trying to provide the lead. Therefore even if it is the case of the male having to tame the shrew, he can only initiate the process, but it is still the female who has to nurture that process. If she doesn't, we have the battle of the sexes.

This is the really difficult part about trying to be a true female, for on the one hand the female must take care not to usurp the power of the male, and on the other hand she has to take care that she does not become the male's doormat. Yet in essence it is not really all that difficult, provided that the female is clear on what she is hoping to achieve. But let us look at an example to help clarify this point.

Consider yourself working as the personal assistant to the Managing Director of a company. Now clearly, if you try to usurp the power of your boss, he will quickly enough put you in your place. However, there will be times when you can see that your boss is struggling with a decision, maybe because he feels inadequate, or not competent enough, or undeserving in some way, or maybe he just feels that he has no right to exercise his seniority towards a specific employee. But if, for whatever reason, your boss is having a hard time in making his decision, you may rest assured that it is not so much a question of him not knowing what to do, but rather that he is struggling to acknowledge to himself what he already knows should be his decision.

Now if your boss trusts you, he will confide in you and share with you his dilemma. But this is where you must take care, for although you are going to have to play the role of mother, you must not make him aware of it, for if you do, he will immediately jump to the conclusion that you think he is weak and in-capable, and will push you away. What in effect you have to do in this case, is somehow to push your boss into taking a stand and making the right decision, but you must do it in such a way that he will feel supported, rather than being given a talking to by mother.

The best way to accomplish this, is for you just to listen very carefully to what your boss is telling you, and then, rather than telling him what to do, just tell him how you feel about his problem. Remember that he has to make the decision. Nevertheless, you can support him enormously by pointing out to him that you believe in him and in his decisions. You can also point out to him that he has the position he holds because others also believe that he is the best man for the job, and that you have little doubt that whatever his decision may be, it will be in the best interests of all concerned. You can even go on to point out to him that he should not worry if his decision upsets some people, for if it is the right decision, then eventually all must benefit, in which case even those who may now be against his decision will in time have to acknowledge his wisdom.

By expressing your confidence in your boss, and your belief in him, you will bring out the very best in that man and, rather than arguing against you, he will begin to listen intently, and in no time at all he will have scraped together enough courage to make the decision he has been trying to duck and dive. Although you would have been mothering your boss in the sense of holding his hand, never once did you try to usurp his power. Instead, you supported him in every way you could. The poor fellow will not even know that you mothered him and indirectly told him what to do. But even if he does see through you, he will only smile quietly to himself and respect you deeply, for your support, and also for your respect in not pointing out to him his moment of weakness. We all have an achilles heel, and we all have our moments of weakness, but we do not need to have our noses rubbed in it.

If you can treat your boss in this manner, I can assure you that you will gain his trust more and more, and it will not be long before he will have elevated you to a position equal to his own within the company. He will still have the position of Managing Director, but there will also be no doubt in anyone's mind that you and your boss are a formidable team, and that the two of you will stand together in mutual support and fight like trojans even against the whole board of directors! You will still be the Managing Director's personal assistant, but more and more will he take you into his confidence, share with you his decisions, and take into account everything you say to him. In this way the male becomes the hunter, yes, but the female is the driving force behind his arrows! For her he will move mountains, and drain the sea!

In this example it is clear to see how great is the influence of the true female within the life of the male. If the truth be told, any male is only as good as the woman in his life can manage to be a true female. In this respect the female again has to go first, for in the final analysis it is her belief in the male that makes of him a true male. This does not imply that a man cannot become a true male without the aid of a female, but it does spell out very clearly that there is only one life, and one awareness with two polarities, one male, one female, and that both polarities are needed for one whole. It is not that the male is more important than the female, or that the male cannot proceed without the support of the female, but it is quite simply that both need each other to exercise intelligent co-operation. And without that intelligent co-operation, neither the male nor the female ever reach their full potential.

In the example we looked at I purposely chose a professional scene, for the reason that it is so much easier to grasp. Yet, know that exactly the same principles are at work within a personal relationship, such as between husband and wife, between brother and sister, or between a mother and her adult son. If the female knows that whatever she is doing is to fulfil her own purpose, her dream, that is, her own dream of having the perfect man in her life, then she can and does feel good about herself in terms of being a female.

Therefore it is not a question of having to stand back for the male because she is inferior in some way, it is simply a question of being highly intelligent in co-operating with the forces of masculinity and femininity. Consequently, irrespective of what the female has to do, whether it is being a personal assistant, a wife, a mother, typing letters, making appointments, washing the dishes or doing the laundry, she knows that she is fulfilling her own dreams by supporting the male in her life, and that because of that support, he will move mountains for her. It is really very much a question of having to make a choice. Do you want to become a second-rate male and do it yourself? Or do you want to be a true female and do it through the male? Both ways you win. But in the first case you will lose your self-respect as a female, and no male will ever really respect you. In the second case you gain your self-respect as a female, and every male around you will flip over backwards to earn from you your respect for him!

In everything we have looked at so far, I think you can begin to see that the female can hardly be termed inferior to the male. Yet, once again the question that comes up here is, "But is the male not being weak in seeking the female's approval?" The answer, as before, is, "No, not really."

The male can only be weak when he does not want to take the lead and therefore, instead of making the decision himself, he expects the female to make the decision for him. Taking support from the female does not weaken the male in any way whatsoever; on the contrary, as we have seen, it enables him to rise to heights he would have found very difficult to negotiate without the female's support. But, having gained that new height, he automatically pulls the female up to join him. That is intelligent co-operation, and intelligent co-operation is a far cry from wanting to hide behind mommy's skirts!

By far the most important point underlying the truth of this myth, is the fact that the female's knowledge is very different to that of the male. Practically speaking, all of the female's knowledge is based upon the concept of support, whereas that of the male is based upon leadership. Here we should remember that knowledge gained through experience is indeed power, for knowledge is something one can use in the moment, and anything that can be used gives one power in one way or another. For example, if you have money in the bank, you have financial power. Likewise, if you have knowledge of politics, you will have political power, should you choose to use that knowledge.

However, whilst knowledge is indeed power, realise also that the power of the female lies in her ability to support the male. But, as with any ability, we either come into this life already showing great talent for developing that ability, or we find that we have to work hard at developing it. Any so-called talent we may have, is very clearly knowledge gained in previous lifetimes, for it stands to reason that knowledge does not just pop into our heads from nowhere, nor do we just suddenly acquire an ability we never had previously. Nevertheless, apart from knowledge gained in previous lifetimes, we can and do also gain new knowledge in this lifetime. We therefore have two types of knowledge, and both of these types together constitute our potential.

So in considering the power, or the knowledge, of the female, we must understand that the only knowledge which can be utilised consciously is that which has been gained in this lifetime. That gained in previous lifetimes may well be considered a natural talent, but until such time as the female concerned can consciously utilise that talent, it remains just beyond her reach. This means that although she will often sense what to do, and how to do it, unless she trusts herself to act upon her feeling, it will be of no good to her. Acting upon her feeling is what I term learning to listen to the heart; something we touched upon earlier, in terms of using one's intuition, or following our gut feel.

This is a most important point, for all too often women do not support the males in their lives, not because they do not want to, but simply because they do not trust their feelings enough to act upon them. Let us look at a few examples.

Say that a woman gets the feeling that her husband is about to make the wrong decision, but, having no concrete proof that she is right, she ends up not voicing her concern. By not voicing her concern, such a woman has not only disempowered herself, but she has also let down her husband when he most needed her support. It is not that she needs to tell him what to do, it is just that by voicing her fear to him she gives him the opportunity to re-evaluate his decision, and so gain a different perspective on it. Therefore, through the act of voicing her concern, the woman is supporting her husband in making the right decision, instead of stepping back for fear that her opinion could be wrong. Even if her opinion is wrong, it still does not matter, for she is not the one making the decision, but her husband. By expressing her opinion, the woman has simply given her husband the opportunity to re-evaluate.

Now consider a woman who gets the feeling that her husband is having an affair, but because she does not have the confidence to confront him with her suspicions, she simply keeps quiet. By keeping quiet, such a woman is inadvertently support-ing her husband in continuing with the affair. If, on the other hand, the woman confronts her husband, she will be supporting him in the sense of forcing him to make the right decisions with respect to their marriage.

Another point that should be mentioned here, concerns the fact that so often the female will come up with feelings that are negative or, at least, appear to be negative. But through not wanting to be negative, or not wanting to sound negative, she will push away these feelings, instead of voicing them. This is clear to see in both of the examples we have looked at here, and yet it is also clear that by feeling bad as a result of her negative feelings, the woman cannot offer the male the support he needs. There is nothing wrong with having nega-tive feelings. Often it is only because of our negative feelings that we can circumvent possible disasters. Therefore, in listening to one's heart, we should never push away our negative feelings. Life does not consist of only positive experiences. So as not to have gaps in our knowledge, and in order to bring out our full potential, we also need negative experiences, and such experiences will always be preceded by negative feelings.

CHAPTER THIRTEEN

MYTH EIGHT

Women should be married

꧁꧂

*T*he real meaning of this myth is that women must be committed. However, this should not be taken at face value, for we must always remember that the only real commitment there is, is commitment to the self. It is simply not possible to be committed to anyone or anything outside of ourselves, for the reason that if we were to try, we would be negating our own freedom.

The whole concept of marriage and commitment boils down to the fact that the two people concerned must be committed to their own inner counterpart, of which the outer partner is a mirror. Consequently, when it is stated that every female should be married, it means that every female must be committed to her own inner male. But, this commitment does not necessarily mean that every woman must be physically married in the accepted sense of the word. What it means is that there must be an inner marriage or, more precisely, a firm commitment between the female and her own inner male. However, the only way in which to learn what this actually means in practice, is to begin by using all outer males as mirrors.

Because of the tremendous difficulty in seeing ourselves objectively, we all need a physical mirror to show us where the opposite polarity of our awareness is at. Yet I stress again that, as we saw in the example of the Managing Director and his personal assistant, this does not necessarily imply a marriage. The reason I keep stressing this point is that people, especially women, so often feel that they are failures unless they have managed to land themselves a spouse in marriage.

None of us can ever realise our full potential unless we can and do co-operate with the opposite polarity of our own awareness, for to be only one polarity means that we are only half a person, and there cannot be something like half a female. You are either a full female, or you are an it! Just like a magnet cannot be a magnet if it has only one polarity, so too can there only be a north pole if there is also a south pole. So it stands to reason that a female can only be a true female if she is married to her polar opposite, that is, committed to her own inner male. In order to have that commitment, the female must also be committed to the mirror of that inner male which, as we know, is the outer male in her life. But this, of course, implies everything we have been looking at so far, and which all boils down to the act of intelligent co-operation.

We would never know how to co-operate with our inner

counterparts if we did not have the opportunity to learn that co-operation with our physical mirrors. Therefore by studying the outer males in her life, the female learns how she relates to them, and how they relate to her. By doing this, the female also learns how to differentiate between the two polarities of her own awareness, and how the two can be made to complement each other.

It is always at this point that the million dollar question will surface: "How do I do that?" Unfortunately there is no way to learn other than through personal experience. People always make the mistake of wanting to know everything up front before they put anything into practice, but life does not work that way. If it did, we would all still be waiting to be born! We only find out how something works once we are doing it. And exactly the same is true here. If you want to know how this works, you are just going to have to use the teachings you are being given in this book to guide you into gaining your own experience. That experience will be your knowledge, and once you have knowledge you will find that there is nothing left to understand! We only seek understanding when we do not yet have the knowledge.

The only real guidance I can give you here, is to say that if you want to know what it means to co-operate with your own inner male, then learn what it is to co-operate with the outer male in your life. If you want to know what it is to be a true female, then study your polar opposite, that is, the male in your life. There is simply no other way. If you want to know what is real peace, then study war. Unless you can see the darkness, you will never know the true meaning of light. Similarly, you will never understand yourself, unless you study your polar opposite. And you will never grasp your own inner male, unless you study your outer male, for just as you cannot see your own face without a mirror, so too will you never get to know your inner male without an outer mirror.

By far the easiest way in which to get started in the right direction, is to begin with your own behaviour. Make a list of all the ways in which you do not use the males in your life as mirrors for your own behaviour, and how, because of that, you do not co-operate with them. If you complete this exercise, you will be amazed to see how quickly you find that you become incapable of blaming the males, for you will come to see that what you are looking at in terms of the males' behaviour, is in actual fact only a reflection of your own lack of co-operation.

Although it may well appear as if I have given you very little in this section with which to work, the truth is that I have in fact given you more than you can digest in one lifetime. By telling you to study the males in your life, to see them as mirrors of your own unknown inner counterpart, and then to seek co-operation with them from what you have learned through your study, is the task of a lifetime! What more do you need? I cannot study for you. I cannot learn on your behalf. Only you can study, learn and seek the required co-operation. And if you do, you will no longer need anyone telling you what to do.

For now you may feel as if you do not know where to begin. But that is not important. Life has no beginning and no end, and therefore we can simply start anywhere at any time. Even if you just sit down and admit to yourself that you are at a loss, then you are already well on your way to learning. How come? Because probably for the very first time in your life you have come to the honest realisation that you have no clue what it means to be a female, or a male, let alone how to seek co-operation with the opposite sex. That in itself is an invaluable realisation, and a very fine state of mind, for unless we come to the point of being able to acknowledge that what we think we know may well be nothing more than a higgledy-piggledy mess of preconceived ideas and prejudices, we remain closed to true learning and to true knowledge.

Therefore do not feel despondent if you feel as if you do not know where to go from here. In not knowing, you have already taken the first step in the right direction – you have opened yourself to finding out, to learning. In being open, you cannot help but to learn, and every new insight, every new bit of experience gained, will lead you one step further, and that step in its turn will reveal the next step, and so on. Just start. How you start is not important. And, above all, remember that under-standing is only for fools who are too lazy to want to learn. Understanding means the ability to grasp information imparted. But it is not information you need here. It is knowledge you need, and knowledge can only be gained through practical experience.

One final word of advice is called for here. If this is the first of my books you are reading, then I suggest that you also read the first book in this series, entitled *This Darned Elusive Happiness*, for in that book I explain the meaning of working with mirrors. I have omitted that section from this book, since it is unnecessary to repeat what has already been explained in another book. In

123

addition to what was explained in that little book, you will also find a great deal more on the concept of mirrors throughout all of my other works. But whatever you do, never forget that the secret of working with mirrors lies in the concept of co-operation, or support, if you prefer. Look into every mirror, and having seen that reflection, allow your heart to guide you in choosing the right values to support. Never support the weaknesses, for if you do, you will serve no-one, least of all yourself. Seek instead to co-operate with your mirrors in such a way that you can and do support the strengths. In short, support the good, the true and the beautiful in your mirrors. If you do that, you will come to find those same qualities within yourself, for our mirrors can never lie! Whatever you see in that mirror, is you!

CHAPTER FOURTEEN

MYTH NINE

Women are sex objects

We come now to the final myth, and the principle it encapsulates, namely, that the female conceives, is the most important by far – all of the previous principles being the necessary steps to arrive at this one. Although I know that it appears as if I am contradicting myself by having stated that the first myth is the most important, there is in actual fact no contradiction as such. Why? Because the first myth and this final myth are two sides of the one coin. The first myth reveals that the female is negative relative to the male, that is, she is the male's polar opposite, and in this final myth we see that the essence of that polarity is conception and childbirth. Therefore this coin, which is the mystery of the female, has two sides, negativity and conception. Let us see what this means, but first we must digress slightly in order to look at the opposite polarity, the male. The necessity and the importance of doing this were explained in the previous chapter.

The male, being the spirit of man made manifest, creates. This is all very well, but realise that to create is a huge responsibility. As we know only too well, it is possible to create all sorts of things. Therefore the male can create chaos or order. He can create happiness or unhappiness. He can create war or peace, wealth or poverty, health or illness, evolution or degeneration, empowerment or disempowerment. In short, the male can create forms which uplift life, or he can create monsters that destroy life.

But, as we have already seen, the female's purpose is to co-operate, to support and to nurture. Do you see the implications here? Do you begin to appreciate the vitally important role of the female in the life of the male? What are you going to support and nurture? That which uplifts? Or that which destroys?

Ah! But now I already hear the clamour in the background! "Why," you ask, "Do I as a female have to support or nurture the male's creations? Why can't I simply support and nurture a creation of my own? After all, anything men can do I can do better, and I sure as hell will not be creating monsters of depravity that destroy life!"

A good question, my friend. But I cannot answer it! Can you? Remember that I did not make men and women, much less males and females. I am only pointing out to you what is. I have no power to change what is. Do you? Nothing stops you from trying. Try as you can. But consider also the cost to you as a female. If you wish to see yourself as a creatress, then by all means create, if you can! But you have not the power to create any more than the male has the power to conceive. You have a womb to conceive, and not a penis with which to impregnate. Medical science can today change the body, but it cannot change the one polarity of awareness into the other. Medical science can change your body into that of a male, but it cannot give you the ability to impregnate, to create!

You may argue and say, "Yes, that is true, but a woman can go out and create her own business, or she can create a piece of art, or she can create a new type of car, or she can create a piece of music, or she can create anything she wishes to create!" And I say, "Yes! That she can. But is it true creation?"

How many women do you know of, who can honestly create something that was never there before? I know of none. Yet there are many women who have nurtured what men have created, and in that nurturing have made it grow into something bigger and better, just as a mother nurtures her children into productive young adults. But it was not the mother who created the children. The mother conceived and gave birth to the children, and then nurtured them into adults. Likewise it is not women who have created business, or art, or cars, or music. Whenever women are involved on the creative side of life, it is to conceive and bring to birth the creations of men.

The female can only sustain and nurture what the male has brought forth with his creative powers. Therefore, when a female starts a business of her own, she is in fact not creating anything new, she is nurturing a practice that already exists.

Similarly, even if the female composes a new piece of music, she will not be creating music; she will only be using existing forms of composition to bring to birth a new piece of music. Yet those forms were not created by females, but by males.

Look at life in terms of it being a game. Call the game chess. Now remember that relative to the spirit of man, we are all female, irrespective of gender. Therefore it is not us, as females, who created life, but the spirit of man. All we can do is to play the game of life. So we move the chess pieces here, and then there, and so we bring to birth many new opportunities that did not exist at the outset of the game. But can we honestly say we are creating? All we are doing is pushing around pieces on a chess board, and through that we are bringing to birth much within the process of life.

Yet, the male does create, for he is totally unlike the female. How come? Simply because the female will instinctively nurture the game and its rules. This is because it is her innermost and undeniable nature to conceive, to bring to birth, and then to nurture. But the male, on the other hand, will instinctively try to understand the game. In doing so he will tamper with the rules, change them, modify them, alter them, until finally he has destroyed the original game. This he does so as to evolve aware-ness through the process of learning, something which is as natural for him as it is to hunt and to kill in order that he and his family may eat and be sustained within the process of life.

Therefore, on the one hand, we have the nurturing of the female which tends towards preservation, and on the other, we have the destruction of the male which tends towards evolution.

Without the male's drive to hunt and kill, he and his family would starve to death, just as without the male's drive towards destruction, the evolution of awareness would become preserved, become frozen in time, and would therefore grind to a halt and die. Yet, without the female's ability to conceive, there would be no family to feed in the first place, just as without her ability to nurture and to preserve, there would be no life left to enhance the evolution of awareness. So once again we see the dual polarity of awareness at work, and how vitally important is the act of intelligent co-operation between the two aspects – male and female.

Destruction versus preservation, male versus female. But realise that destruction is very much the act of creation, as para-doxical as this appears to be. It is simply not possible to create something out of nothing. In order to create anything we need building blocks of sorts, and material for these must come from somewhere. This is not a concept I want to explore in any depth in this book, for it is possible to write volumes on just this one concept. Therefore let it suffice to say that if we are going to create, we must first tear from out of the fabric of life itself the material with which to create something new. The implications of this are quite clear, namely, that in order to create we must destroy something else. An obvious example of this is the act of procreation.

When a man impregnates a woman, he has not simply ejaculated sperm, as so many ignorant fools are prone to believe. Although it is true that the mere ejaculation of sperm is a per-fectly harmless excretion of bodily fluid, the act of impregnation is a totally different kettle of fish altogether. The moment a man impregnates a woman, he has, through the medium of his sperm, torn from out of his own electromagnetic being a small portion of his life-essence. It is that portion of his life-essence that forms the one polarity of a nucleus of new life within the now fertilised ovum of the woman. However, it is not only his own electromagnetic being which the male has damaged in this process. That portion of his life-essence, within the woman's ovum, also acts as a magnetic force which tears its opposite polarity away from the female's electromagnetic being, for both polarities are needed for conception to take place. But quite apart from this damage the male has caused to both himself and the woman, he has in addition also destroyed her virginity, and has started up a whole new metabolic structure within her body.

Nevertheless, there is destruction and then there is destruction. There is the type of wanton destruction that does not support either life or the evolution of awareness, and then there is the type of destruction that upholds life, uplifts it, and aids in the evolution of awareness, as for example in the act of procreation. But even here, we need to take care, for just as the act of procreation can be abused in terms of rape, plunder and indiscriminate breeding, so too can we turn any good act into something which is foul and wantonly destructive.

Not only does the male produce and ejaculate the life-giving sperm, but so too does he produce and spew forth the germ of all forms. The female, on the other hand, provides the egg. By receiving the sperm inside of her, that egg becomes impregnated, after which her womb nurtures and finally brings to birth the new form that was created during the act of intelligent co-operation between her and the male.

Conception and childbirth are therefore very much the male's responsibility, just as it is his responsibility to see to it that only those forms which are beneficial to the evolution of awareness are created. However, as is only too clear to see in the world today, men shun that responsibility, because they refuse to acknowledge that the act of creation is their responsibility. Nowhere is this clearer to see than in that form created by men, and termed sexual promiscuity.

By not taking responsibility for the creative act of procreation, men have pushed that responsibility, their responsibility, onto the woman. As a result, men feel that they are at liberty to sow their wild oats around indiscriminately and even to rape, for in their minds the female body is there for their fun, for their gratification, and for the fulfilment of their sexual lust. But, in their efforts not to be constantly pregnant and not to give birth to every Tom, Dick and Harry's offspring, women have inadvertently co-operated with men in the creation of that cruel form. By assuming responsibility which is not their's, women now mostly take the infamous pill, and thereby keep their bodies in a perpetual false pregnancy!

Sad and ironic, is it not? In trying to be incorporated into the world of the male, and in taking the lead of men who are nothing but spoilt and highly irresponsible little boys, women the world over have had to sacrifice their self-respect through learning to live a lie. In trying to be accepted within the world of the male, and in trying to please and to gratify, these women are playing a role, and have even convinced themselves that they are happy to have their bodies abused. If the man has set the example that his wild oats are for all and sundry, then why should the woman not spread her legs for every dickhead that comes along and wants to climb on top?

Be that as it may, sexual promiscuity is all a lie. A terrible lie breeding more and more confusion. Yet, confusion is the name of the game it seems! "Here, just swallow this pill. It will confuse the natural functions of your body, just as men have confused your mind! But at least in that confusion your body will not conceive, for it thinks it is already pregnant, and in that blurry haze of confusion between one sexual partner and another, you will also not have to conceive the purpose of any of these jerks!"

But in spite of all the confusion, in spite of the woman's denial of her own self-respect, she still finds herself conceiving and nurturing a purpose which is now rapidly beginning to destroy everything that has always been held sacred within the act of procreation. This abuse of the sexual act is no different, in fact, to the abuse men are inflicting upon everything else in the world.

War, famine, illness, unhappiness and poverty, are all the results of the various types of forms brought forth out of man's sense of greed, just as his insatiable greed for sex has brought forth broken relationships, venereal disease, AIDS and prostitutes. By submitting to their greed, instead of taking responsibility for their creative powers, men have plundered the planet's natural resources in exactly the same way as they have forced their sexual lust upon women. Even in this day and age, and not only in a few cultures, are women still forced into having to give birth to one child after another, whether their wombs can handle it or not, whilst at the same time being made to work like slaves, and often being beaten up for not having pleased the man in some way. Likewise, do men still cut down whole forests, and then wonder why it no longer rains, and destroy vast tracks of land with indiscriminate farming practices, and then wonder why the soil is becoming infertile. But then, if forests are there for men to plunder, then why not females too? If the land is there for men to rape, then why not rape females too?

Oh! I know! There are today certain moves towards nature conservation, just as there are certain moves towards the protection of the female's rights. But who is going to protect the planet and nature from a form of self-destruction that has been created by men? And who is going to protect the female from a form of self-destruction also created by men? If it no longer rains when and where it should, and if the ozone layer is breaking up, who are the men that will change this? And if females today are only too happy to have a hysterectomy just so that they do not have to endure the messy business of menstruation, and to be sterilized so that they can enjoy sex freely without having to swallow a pill, then who are the men that will change this?

But still, in spite of all of this, none of us can afford to play the blame game. Therefore let us in fairness look also at the female's responsibility in all of this mess. Realise that at the end of the day any creation is a sexual act, no matter whether it is an invention, a musical composition or a baby. But even though creation is the male's responsibility, we must also not forget that no man can create without the female's ovum and her womb. Accordingly, the female too must take responsibility for accepting the male's sperm, for taking his lead, and ultimately for supporting and nurturing his purpose.

If the rights of women are to be protected and restored in the true sense of the word, and if the rights of that greater female we term the planet are also to be protected, then it is time that men the world over start growing up fast, and stop playing around like so many spoilt little boys taking revenge on mother. But so too must women the world over start taking responsibility for supporting men to claim their power as true males who can, and must, take the lead in rectifying mistakes that are crippling everyone and everything. No longer can women afford not to discriminate wisely, for they have to learn to think for themselves, and to make up their minds whether or not the men in their lives are wanting to create forms which uplift, or forms which destroy.

There is absolutely no need for women to prostitute themselves and their values to a purpose which violates their female sense of what constitutes the right values in life. No female has to conceive, and no female has to give birth to a creation she cannot believe in. If the female lends herself to the male's creation, whether this is the sexual act, or any other act of creation, then it must be because she believes in that male's purpose, and therefore wants to support that purpose, and wants to co-operate with him in the creations brought forth by that purpose.

The question every female should ask herself is, "Do I want this male as a mirror of my own inner counterpart?" Ask yourself if he shows you the respect he should have for the mirror of his own inner female. Ask yourself if he treats you with the same respect he should be showing to the world around him. Does he hunt only so that he may feed his family? Or does he hunt just for the fun of killing? Does he share with you his purpose, or does he only share with you his sexual lust?

Look, and see for yourself, if the man in your life is truly taking responsibility for the sexual act. By this I am not just referring to the physical act, but to all of his creative acts. The true male does not share only his physical sperm with the female – he shares with her also all of his creative essence at all levels of their relationship – physical, emotional and mental. It is simply not possible for any female to exercise intelligent co-operation with a man who does not share his emotions, his feelings, his thoughts, ideas, fears, doubts, hopes, desires, wishes, dreams and, in short, his everything. If he remains a closed book and only wants to share in the physical act of sex, then it is impossible for the female to conceive his purpose at any level other than the physical act of procreation.

Men who are closed do not incorporate the female into their lives. Their attitude is simply one of wanting to use the female as some sort of glorified servant who also has to satisfy his sexual needs. But servants do not share in the life of the master. Nor are servants expected to conceive his purpose or his child. For such men, the female's only real purpose is to clean up after him, and that includes seeing to it that she does not conceive and bring to birth anything he may in a moment of "abandonment" have shared with her, irrespective of whether it is an idea, a dream, a fear, or his sperm. Such a man expects that you will accept his seed but, in keeping to your role as servant, will not conceive. Even at the physical level, such men are quite happy to leave contraception to the female. But realise that if you are having to contracept the male's sperm, then you are more than likely also contracepting him at all other levels within your relationship.

It is just a fact that no true female can respect a man who is not taking responsibility for being a male, and where there is no respect, you will, even with the best will in the world, not conceive his purpose, physically, emotionally or mentally. Neither will you be supporting him, no matter how much you think you are, or how much you think you may love him. In this respect, remember that true support is the act of intelligent co-operation, and it has nothing to do with supporting the weaknesses and the lack of responsibility.

Therefore, if it is this man's weakness you are supporting, then be honest enough to acknowledge to yourself that you are nothing except his servant or, worse still, his servant-whore! If it is a servant or whore you wish to be, then go right ahead and support him in his indulgence, but then also be brave enough to accept the consequences of your prostitution. It is said that many a true word is spoken in jest, and nowhere is this clearer to see than in that vulgar expression men so often use, namely, "it's fucked up," meaning that it has been abused to the point of uselessness. The problem is that people rarely, if ever, pay attention to the truths which they utter. Are you willing to be honest? Are you willing to allow yourself to become fucked up?

Be honest with yourself. Make a list of all the ways in which you allow the men in your life to destroy not only you, but also the world around them. Look to see whether you provide the male in your life with a counterbalance, and how. In other words, if he is busy destroying, are you willing to confront him on the issue honestly? Look also to see if you complement the male in every respect, that is, if the male in your life is being creative, are you supporting him in that creation, or are you supporting him in being wantonly destructive? And finally, look to see if, and how, you are supporting the male in claiming his power. In relation to this it should be a question of, "Are you supporting him to claim his power as a true male, and as a creator, or are you helping him to escape taking responsibility for the creative act?"

PART THREE

Getting to know yourself as a female

CHAPTER FIFTEEN

Role models

❧❧❧

That which is learned at the knee
of our parents creates a lasting impression.

I n the preceding chapters we attempted to gain an understanding of the implications of what it is to be female, and why it is that so many women fail to bring out their full potential as females. Now that you have at least some clarity, you are half-way there. Once we can see what it is we are doing wrong, we can start to change our ways, our behaviour and our approach, and once we do that, we are well on our way to success.

We have already touched upon the all-important concept of self-discipline; remember that everything we have looked at so far can only really be achieved through exercising self-discipline. Therefore we now need to look at this concept in greater depth.

Self-discipline is mainly acquired in two principal ways. First, we learn basic discipline from our mothers, in the form of what may be termed the basic values in life. And secondly, we learn discrimination from our fathers. By "discrimination" I am referring to the ability to take out of life what is useful and beneficial, or in other words, the ability to choose between that which is constructive and that which is destructive.

Although we can learn to become disciplined at any point in our lives, it is by far the best to learn this when we are still small children, because, generally speaking, it is only what we have learned as a young child that tends to stick and to become second nature. It is, of course, exactly for this reason that the habits of a lifetime are so very difficult to eradicate, for if you have never learned self-discipline, then it is really rather difficult to learn it later on in life.

As we have already noted, the people we learn from most are our parents, and it is not so much what they tell us, but rather what they show us through example. All children will normally base their behaviour patterns upon those of their parents, because they have taken them as role models. In using our parents as role models there are three major factors that come into play. Firstly, respect for mother; secondly, hero worship of father; and thirdly, the warmth and nurturing we received from both of our parents. Let us look at these three factors more closely.

It is always at the knee of the mother that the young child learns the basic values of life. These values are inevitably in the nature of respect – respect for food, respect for clothing, respect for money, for animals, for friends, for a home, for cleanliness, for discipline in general and, in short, respect for life. However,

141

by far the most important value a girl learns from her mother, is respect for the male.

The basic values a child learns from its mother obviously depend very much upon the respect its mother has for all around her, and also upon the child's respect for its mother. Here we should note that the word "respect" means "to look again", meaning that the world is not what it appears to be, and therefore that we cannot afford to take things at face value, or for granted. This is especially important in relation to the male, because a girl will always end up emulating her mother, just as a boy will emulate his father. Therefore if the girl's mother is a doormat, the girl will become a doormat, and if her mother has no respect for the male, then the girl too will have no respect for the males in her life.

The father plays a very different role in the life of a child, for invariably Dad is out working most of the day, and so, when he is at home, he is always looked upon as being the loving provider who is also the big, strong, brave defender. As a result, any child tends to hero worship its father, and the really exciting part of the day is when Dad comes home. Furthermore, Dad always seems to have an answer for anything that happened during the day, and since he is the one who normally sorts out all disputes in a way which everyone can live with, he is also looked upon as being the wise one in the family. It is therefore mainly from the father that children learn discrimination, provided, of course, that Dad is a true male. We are not here referring to the guy who arrives home at ten o'clock at night, drunk out of his mind and then beats up his wife before raping her. We're talking about the average male who is trying his best to be a husband and a father.

Even if mother is a doormat and father is a drunk, as children, we still learn everything we need to learn by using them as role models, irrespective of whether they are positive or negative models. In this respect it does not matter if we learn how to do something, or if we learn how not to do something. Either way we learn, and therefore we always have the right parents, whatever we may think of them. However, for the sake of simplicity, we are going to look at only the average parents.

A most important point to bear in mind, is that the discrimination we learn from father does, of course, always pivot around the basic values we learn from mother. This is so very important because, in learning how to cope with life in general, the female can only meet the demands of life through her ability to discriminate in terms of what has value or not. In fact, all that self-discipline really boils down to, is the female's knowledge of basic values, and her skill at being able to discriminate between many different values.

However, in order to learn these two aspects of self-discipline, it is also vital that the child grows up in a home in which she receives ample warmth and nurturing. If the child does not grow up with this love, she will not respect either parent. In such a case the child will still use the parents as role models, but instead of using them in a positive sense, she will use them as role models in the negative sense. This means that the child will grow up acting out what she feels her parents are doing to her.

CHAPTER SIXTEEN

The over-dominant mother

❧

In looking at our parents we should take care not to take them at face value. For example, over-dominant women fall mainly into two categories. In the first category we have the proverbial battle-axe who makes no bones about the fact that she is the boss, and in the second category we find women who often appear to be meek and mild, but who actually have backbones of steel. Being mild and meek is only a behaviour which allows them to manipulate everyone around them, yet if you scratch a little beneath that outer facade, you will find a woman who is every bit as hard as nails. This is not to say that all women who are meek and mild are over-dominant. Some of these women will be genuine doormats who are just too weak to stand up and fight for their rights. In such cases, the driving force behind these women is usually a severe self-hatred, causing them to believe that they deserve no better.

Now, the girl who grows up with an over-dominant mother will usually end up manifesting three very distinct forms of behaviour. Firstly, she has a resistance to being contained; secondly, she wants to wear the pants; and thirdly, she is highly ambitious. Let us look at each of these three forms of behaviour more closely.

In having a resistance to being contained, the woman will have no real respect for men. Such a woman will also always want to be right, and so will be quick to become highly defensive and indignant. In addition she will also be rather rigid in her thinking and, as a result, will often be very reluctant to make changes in her life. However, if forced to make changes, such a woman will then often act impulsively, in the sense of not first considering the possible consequences of her acts. These women are also quite often careless about their appearance, in that they cannot be bothered very much about their hair, their make-up, or clothing, and their homes too will often reflect that same carelessness. By "carelessness" I am not necessarily referring to a mess, but rather to a lack of care in detail, finesse and beauty.

The women who want to wear the pants are those who are very much the boss. Always wanting to be right, and always wanting to tell everyone what to do, when to do it and where to do it, these women cannot resist mothering everyone in sight, irrespective of whether it is a child, a male, a dog or a parrot. Generally speaking such women take responsibility for everything, and will always insist that they know best and are therefore in charge of everything, including the finances, the bond on the house and the monthly accounts. But they are also quick to pass the buck should something go wrong, and if a man is around he will be the first to get the blame. In addition, they are also very domineering and cannot resist the challenge to compete against males, for they are for ever convinced that males are somehow inferior to women. Needless to say, these women tend to look upon femininity as being a sign of weakness, and therefore something to be avoided at all costs.

Being ambitious, these particular women tend to be very logical and so not only lack imagination, but also tend to suppress true creativity, in the sense of, "Let's not have any competition around here. I'm the boss, Okay?" For women such as these it is very important that they and everyone else should conform to what they perceive as being the norm. Being so very bossy, they have a rather staid sense of humour, and find it difficult to laugh at the folly of life.

In what we have looked at in this chapter, I have, for the sake of simplicity, painted only the worst case scenario. Obviously every individual is different, and therefore no two people will manifest their behaviour in the same way, nor will they have the same approach towards life. Also, bear in mind that although I have listed all of the behaviour patterns that emerge as a result of having had an over-dominant mother, mothers too are unique and individual. As a result, your mother will not necessarily display all of these traits, and since you are different to your mother, you may also not necessarily have all of the characteristics listed here. Nevertheless, the potential for these traits will always be there, and even if they are not obvious now, they may well become manifested at some later stage in life.

What's more, none of us like to show our negative traits. Consequently, we have all learned to mask these characteristics so that they appear normal and therefore acceptable, or alternatively, we have masked them in such a way that they appear to be something completely different to what they really are. Yet, if you are prepared to be honest with yourself, you will be able to see the true nature of all your characteristics.

I have chosen to put the accent on the over-dominant mother, for this is what the majority of women are, since most men in the world today, as in the past, are still very much little boys. Nonetheless, we must also briefly consider the mother who is genuinely weak and a doormat, and the resulting influence this type of behaviour has upon her daughters.

The woman who has grown up with a doormat for a mother is not difficult to spot. Being incredibly shy and withdrawn, such women are not only introverted, but also come across as being timid to the point of being pale, colourless, and in short, rather dull and uninteresting. Although they can often be quite pretty if they would only take greater care of themselves, these women are very prone to self-neglect due to anorexia in the early stages of life, and sometimes also alcohol abuse in their latter years.

Having an almost non-existent self-image, these women also have hardly any self-respect and, as a result, are insecure to the point of doubting and dithering in everything, apparently having no real opinion of their own, and coming across as being somewhat dumb, even though they can have perfectly good minds.

147

Easily frightened by everything, these women also tend to succumb very quickly to the mentality of the proverbial victim, calling forth one incredible disaster after another in their lives. For example, if they are not raped by strangers, then they get raped by their brothers, their fathers and even their husbands. If they do not crash their own cars, then someone else does it for them, after having stolen it. If they contract a disease, it is either a very rare disease, or one not ever heard of before. If they go shopping, the store burns down and they are trapped in the cold-room for hours on end. And so on, and so on! For ever victims, and for ever hard-done-by, such women spend their lives feeling very sorry for themselves. In short, life is a total bitch, and people like me writing such terrible things about them must obviously hate them! Cry! Cry! Sob! Sob! Wring hands in despair!

CHAPTER SEVENTEEN

The weak father

The weak father is a man who does not believe in his own maleness. He therefore finds life much easier when he hides behind his wife's skirts, often looking deep into the bottle, and talking up a storm that is nothing more than hot air! Being weak, such a man has very little intention of standing up for himself, simply because such a bold action is much too threatening for him. Yet, care must be taken not to assume that if you had a dominant mother, you will automatically have a weak father. Being genuinely weak is a far cry from pretending to be weak – something which most men love to indulge in, for in this way they too can manipulate everyone around them. I wish to point this out here because, although the world has always been, and is still riddled by weak men, very few of these men are genuinely weak. If pushed far enough, a real bull suddenly emerges! Nevertheless, irrespective of whether the man really is weak, or just pretends to be weak, the effects upon his daughters are the same.

The girl with a weak father, or a father who pretends to be weak, will end up manifesting once again three distinct forms of behaviour. These are characterised by, firstly, a sense of being disillusioned with life; secondly, a sense of being disappointed in general; and thirdly, an over-emphasis of sexuality.

The sense of disillusionment manifests primarily in terms of general apathy, often in the sense of being "helpless" and "lost." Growing out of this apathy is an attitude of "I don't know what to do." As a result, these women are prone to procrastination, to complaining about not having enough time for themselves, and that most things are a burden. Also, such women often lack self-respect, even though they are normally vociferous in demanding respect from others. However, because they lack self-respect, and therefore any real sense of honour, they always complain about feeling unacknowledged in some way. In trying to get the recognition they long for, these women are extremely good at scheming and manipulating, even though they are not always conscious of the implications of their actions.

The sense of being disappointed tends to come out mainly as being evasive and cautious. This is very much in the sense of "once bitten, twice shy." Through being careful not to expose themselves to possible emotional hurt, such women are normally very insensitive people who can also become rather abusive in both their speech and manner, especially towards men. These women also lack commitment, but can cover for this by being loud and all-knowing, thereby very much putting on an act of "I'm okay." In addition, they also tend towards being somewhat moody at the best of times, and hyper-sensitive most of the time.

The over-emphasis of sexuality is first manifested in the early years in terms of competing against the mother to try to get the father's attention and approval. Later that sense of competing against is extended to include all other females, but it is still geared towards winning the male's attention. Such women then become very flirtatious, and even obsessed with the sexual act. Consequently, they will often exhibit seductive behaviour of which they appear to be quite oblivious, and yet they will not really try too hard to cover up for behaviour that is quite clearly promiscuous. If the obsession with sexuality is allowed to get out of hand, it is not uncommon for these women to start exhibiting even lesbian tendencies.

There is little point in considering the influences of the strong father, simply because if you had a strong father, he would have been a true male, in which case your mother would have been a true female, and you would not now be feeling the need to read this book. Yet, remember what was mentioned in the previous chapter – no two men, and no two fathers, are the same. Every individual is unique, as is his behaviour, and every girl will have her own reaction to her father's behaviour. Thus, even sisters from the same family and with the same father and mother, can and do grow up as different individuals, exhibiting different characteristics. Just remember that the characteristics we are looking at are potentials which are common to all, and those potentials can manifest at any time in life, and under a great many guises.

CHAPTER EIGHTEEN

Hunting for power

Having gained a better perspective on who and what you are, in terms of your behaviour patterns, we now need to return to the concept of self-discipline, to see how this relates to nurturing. Remember that the principal role of the female is to nurture and to support. But, as we have already noted, any support given must be honest support, and must therefore be free from bias, whether positive or negative. However, to be capable of such honesty requires not only self-respect, but also a great deal of self-discipline.

Self-discipline for the female means being a disciple of her own inner male. Here it is important to keep in mind that the male represents the spirit, and that the female can only come into her own right if and when the male incorporates her into his world, in the sense that he must include the unknown into the known. To be a disciple of the inner male means that the female must take the lead of the outer male in her life, and she does this in two ways. Firstly, she entices the male into taking her as his disciple; and, secondly, she uses her knowledge to nurture his purpose. What in effect this boils down to, is that the female must know how to hunt the male, and how to relate to his purpose.

In practice it will be found that very few young men ever know what their purpose in life is meant to be. Not yet having enough life's experience to draw from, and taking much longer to mature than women, most young adult men are normally quite vague about the more serious side of life. Since he is quite content at this stage in his life simply to dream and explore, it takes the female's more mature insight to fathom what the young man's purpose in life really is. But, as is so clear to see, this is very much mother's intuition we are referring to here, and unless such a young lady is careful in how she goes about it, she will find her young prince running away from her as soon as she wants to start telling him what to do with his life!

The way in which evolution has set it up is that the male is the hunter in the outer world, but the female is the hunter in the inner world, which includes also all issues pertaining to the home and personal relationships. This does not mean that the female excludes the outer world. However, she will always bring back to the home, or inner world, whatever she encounters in the outer world, as a result of her hunting endeavours there. This concept will become clearer in the following chapters. But what do we really mean by "hunting?" Put quite simply, it means the acquisition of knowledge gained through personal experience, and as we have already noted much earlier, such knowledge is in reality power – power which we can use in fulfilling our fate, and also in the acquisition of even more power. But, for the sake of clarity, let us see what this means in practical terms.

In hunting for power, the female involves herself in five areas of endeavour, but with a two-fold purpose in mind. One, the female strives for the acquisition of power through the medium of her own inner world; and two, she strives to achieve freedom within the context of the outer world, or the world "out there" beyond the confines of her home and personal relationships.

When she hunts for power within her inner world, the female gains knowledge in five cardinal areas of endeavour. These are sobriety, action, feeling, warmth and intent. Sobriety is the ability to assess every situation in one's life precisely as to its true value. It is often called clarity, and it is a vital quality, since we cannot take action in our lives without being clear on our circumstances and values. Such an ability implies having to be ruthless in the sense that one has to stand detached from emotion, and not allow personal feelings to cloud the issue at hand. Sobriety does not mean having to be heartless, but it does mean that we have to be honest and objective, even if the truth does hurt! Sobriety is a quality of awareness which is very much based upon knowledge that is certain, and in this respect it is worth noting that the only worthwhile changes we bring about are those made with sobriety.

Action speaks for itself, but it is good to bear in mind that by action, we are referring to the implementation of that type of decision which propels us forward in our search for happiness and fulfilment of purpose. It is therefore not action as in action in the gym, or action in cleaning the house, or action on the dance floor that we are talking about here. It is the action that brings about meaningful change in our lives that is important.

Feeling, we have already discussed, and we saw that it primarily means gut feel, or intuition. It is the ability to participate in all of life freely, without the restraints imposed by logical assumption, and it can only be corroborated through experience.

Warmth is the nurturing aspect of the human being, and is an act that supplies the care needed by any living thing to grow, to flourish and to prosper. Intent, on the other hand, is the ability to focus on what is most important to you in your life at any given moment, irrespective of whether it is to nurture a new seedling in your garden, to nurture the dream of having your own home, or to nurture the belief that the man in your life will claim his power as a true male. In other words, nurturing pertains very much to the physical care of someone or something, but intent means that you keep your focus on what you want, and because of that, you do everything within your power to materialise that wish.

When she hunts for freedom in the outer world, the female likewise involves herself in five areas of activity, namely, education, politics, medicine, religion and science. But so as to avoid preconceived ideas, and falling into the trap of taking these pursuits at face value, let us look briefly at each in turn.

It is quite obvious to see how education leads to freedom, because unless we have an education, we can never really be free in the sense of being our own boss. However, care should be taken not to see education only in terms of academic schooling. Academic schooling is part of being educated, but true education means that we have acquired ability the to handle life and the many challenges it brings us. Unless we have that education we will end up being beggars, and beggars can't be choosers.

Politics more or less speaks for itself, because only a little thought is required to see that the sole purpose of politics concerns the ability to negotiate for strategies that allow for the manipulation of power. In other words, we look to see what it is we would like, and then we decide how best to interact with others in achieving our goal. This can be as simple as telling the butcher that unless he can give you a better price you will be forced to buy from his competitor. Or it can be a subtle as telling the school principal that you would love to bake some cakes for the school fête, but unless the mathematics teacher can give your son some extra attention in mathematics you are going to have to spend extra time coaching him at home, and therefore will not have the time to bake cakes. Alternatively it can be as complicated as having to support the tennis club, whose president also serves on the town planning council, so that you can use your influence there to lobby for new street lights in your area. Yet the bottom line of all this type of endeavour is politics, leading to that freedom which enables one to materialise one's own wishes.

Medicine implies the freedom from disease, but bear in mind that we are here referring, not so much to physical diseases, but to that dis-ease caused by an imbalance of sorts. Therefore, medicine in its broadest sense includes also the female's concern with relationships, irrespective of what type of relationship this may be. For example, if her child is struggling with his maths, she looks at the relationship between her son and his teacher, as well as at the relationship with her son and his school. Likewise, if the meat is too expensive, she is very much looking at her relationship with her butcher. But in both cases she will be looking at those relationships in terms of how best to overcome the disease.

Religion is not at all what it appears to be at face value. By religion I am implying the true meaning of religion, which has nothing at all to do with man's sense of separativeness based upon prejudice. By religion I am referring to the human being's innate drive towards understanding him– or herself relative to the meaning and purpose of life. It is therefore very much to do with building an awareness of ourselves in relation to life, for this is the true meaning of religion, namely, "relating back to the self." In practice this means ridding ourselves of our social conditioning, and thus achieving our freedom.

Science very much speaks for itself, in that the purpose of science is not only to enhance the quality of all of life, but also to uncover information which everyone can use in achieving freedom through the medium of technology, irrespective of whether this is medical technology, mechanical technology, educational technology, or food technology.

Having explained the two-fold approach of the female in hunting for power, let us now consider how this actually works in practice, especially the concept of the female hunting for power in the world at large. To do so, we will look at a few examples.

If Mary comes to realise that there is a lack of sobriety within her life, she immediately turns within to start searching for possible solutions, or answers, to what could be wrong. In other words, she starts to look at her behaviour to see what it is that is causing the confusion, and therefore, lack of clarity. In this particular case, Mary is hunting for power entirely within the scope of her own inner world.

If, on the other hand, Mary senses that her son is experiencing a lack of clarity in his mathematics, she now has to turn her attention to the outer world. Obviously her endeavour here is going to be centred around education. In order to find the sobriety she needs in order to help her son, she will start to question whether the educational system her child is following is actually fulfilling its purpose. If she feels that it is not doing so, then once again Mary has no option other than to turn within, to start looking at what she feels is wrong with the system, and how best to solve her son's problem.

The important point to grasp here is that, irrespective of whether the female is hunting for power within or without, she is always having to resort back to her feelings, and therefore to her own inner world. As a result, the true female only uses her endeavours within the outer world in order to relate to those inner aspects of herself she would otherwise not encounter. Therefore, once again we see that the female is only ever concerned with her inner world, and, figuratively speaking, in tending to the hearth, even when she interacts with the outer world.

Furthermore, because it is the male who is concerned with hunting for power in the outer world, once Mary has found the sobriety she needs, and has thereby established what the problem is concerning her son's difficulties with mathematics, she will hand the challenge over to her husband. As the female, it is not Mary's responsibility to tackle the school principal on the issue of education. Instead she will present her husband with what she has uncovered, and then stand back in the sense of allowing him, as the male, to decide what action is to be taken. Since it is the male's responsibility to deal with the world at large, and since he is well equipped to do so, Mary must leave him to sort out the problem from there.

To understand this even better, let us rework the same example, but from a slightly different angle. Say that Sean, Mary's husband, expresses his concern to Mary about their son's marks at school. Now if Mary is a true female, the first thing she will do is to use her discrimination to pinpoint what exactly is causing Sean's concern about their son, Johnny. Are Johnny's marks suddenly much lower than they have always been on average? Are all of Johnny's marks equally low? Is Johnny always doing his homework, and how conscientiously? Is Johnny complaining about his schoolwork? And so on, and so on. But in all of this Mary is very much concentrating on what is happening on the home-front, that is, within her own world.

Now if, having looked at all these possibilities, Mary comes to the conclusion that the problem does not originate with Johnny, then she will start to look at the outer world. If she finds that the problem lies there, she will once again turn back into her own

159

inner world, to search there for the answers as to what exactly constitutes the problem. Once she has come up with something definite, Mary will share her findings with Sean.

However, even when the female has been able to identify the problem, it often happens that she will not be able to pinpoint or express it exactly, not because she is stupid or incapable, but simply because the true female relies much more on gut feeling than on rationality to find the sobriety she is seeking. Therefore it will not be strange if Mary tells Sean that she believes the problem lies in how Johnny is being educated at school, or that she feels Johnny is not very happy with his teacher, or that she feels he is perhaps not communicating well with his teacher.

The point here is that the female will often just give the male all sorts of feelings, but will hand it over to him to ascertain what those feelings translate into in terms of practicalities. This is especially true if the issue concerns the outer world. So, if Mary feels that Johnny is not doing his homework properly, she does not think what that translates into in terms of practicalities, she simply follows her feelings in sorting out both Johnny and his problems regarding his schoolwork, for this is very much her domain and her world. However, if the problem lies outside of her domain, Mary will still give Sean her feelings, but she will then leave it to him to think out how best to handle the education of his son in the world out there. Therefore, when the female works in the world at large, it is only in the sense of being able to find the necessary direction she needs in order to go into the unknown of her own inner being, and to find there what is needed.

Remember that finding direction, and searching within the unknown, are both actions which require the use of the mind and, as we know, this entails the act of discrimination. But, as we saw so clearly in the second example of Johnny, Mary is using her discrimination to support the male's purpose, in this case, by using her discrimination to find the knowledge Sean needs so that they can help their son. This, in the final analysis, is the true meaning of nurturing, that is, nurturing the purpose of the male.

CHAPTER NINETEEN

The female perspective on relationships

❧

If the female is to practise the concepts we looked at in the previous chapter correctly, it is vital that we understand what they really mean. In this respect we must always bear in mind that all of life is but a system of relationships, and that relationships for the female pivot around nurturing and relating to the purpose of the male. Therefore let us look at how relationships fit into this scheme.

Looking again at the five areas of endeavour, we see that within her own private world, whether this is her inner state of being, or her home environment, the female is hunting for power in terms of sobriety, action, feeling, warmth and intent.

Sobriety entails the art of listening. By learning to listen, instead of constantly wanting to be listened to, the true female learns to take, rather than for ever wanting to give, like the mother, irrespective of whether this is giving food, giving love, giving attention, or giving advice. By learning to take, the true female takes the male's lead, takes the direction he has pointed out, and above all, she takes his purpose as her own.

Action implies the art of discrimination. Discrimination for the female does not necessarily mean having to find solutions to problems, but it does mean that she uses her mind to try and fathom out what the need of the male really is. By taking this action, she can and does provide him with all the information he may need, either to find solutions to the challenges of the moment, or to decide what their next move forward must be.

Feeling is the art of entering the unknown. By learning to listen to her gut feel, the female listens to her heart in order to use the irrational knowledge called forth through her interaction with the unknown. Here it is important to remember that the unknown is exactly that; the unknown. In facing anything which is unknown the mind is useless. The only way we can handle the unknown, is to feel our way in the dark, by using the gut or the intuition.

Warmth is the art of nurturing, and it is closely allied with intent, the art of conception. Know that we cannot nurture something we do not have. If it is a hope we wish to nurture, we must first have that hope. If it is a child we wish to nurture, we must first have that child. And if it is the male's purpose we want to nurture, we must first know what that purpose is. But from the perspective of the female, to have is to conceive, irrespective of whether it is the conception of a hope, a baby, or the male's purpose. Therefore intent for the female is very much centred around intending conception. For example, if the female wants the man in her life to become a real male by claiming his power, then, as the expression states it so well, "to all intents and purposes," the female conceives the concept of the true male.

When she is hunting in the outer world for that power which leads to freedom, the true female looks upon education in its broadest possible sense as being the art of recapitulation. This involves the necessity not only to recall, but also to correlate, all of our life's experience into one meaningful whole that we can rightfully term knowledge, or power. In this regard, recapitulation is vital in the acquisition of sobriety.

Politics has everything to do with what I like to term the art of stalking, irrespective of whether it is someone else we are stalking, or ourselves. By stalking, I am, of course, referring to manipulation, except that I like to differentiate between plain manipulation and stalking. Plain manipulation is an act which is so designed that only you are going to win, and for your own self-centred purposes, whereas stalking is an act designed so that both you and your opponent can win.

Through stalking you still get to win, but not at the expense of the other person, even though it will often be at the expense of their behaviour. For example, and looking again at our previous examples in politics, if you use threats to make the butcher give you a better price for your purchases, you will have manipulated him for your own self-centred gain. But if you stalk the school principal into finding out why Johnny is struggling with his mathematics, which you will have done by dropping the hint about the cakes and the school fête, the chances are that he will look into the matter, in which case you win, Johnny is likely to win, and the school principal will get his cakes! In this example you have stalked the school principal so that everyone wins – even the mathematics teacher, for in being questioned by the principal as to why Johnny is not doing well in his mathematics, the teacher now has the opportunity to upgrade his teaching methods.

As an example of what is meant by stalking ourselves, consider the meaning of reacting, as opposed to acting. If you find that no matter how hard you try, you always end up mothering the male in your life, then clearly you need to take a long hard look at your behaviour. If you do, the chances are that you will soon come to the realisation that the problem lies in the fact that you keep on reacting out of habit, instead of acting in such a way that you get the desired results. To stop this pattern you will have to teach yourself to be sufficiently detached, so that you can observe every situation as if you were merely a witness. Only in this way will you gain the necessary objectivity to see your behaviour patterns for what they are, to stop your normal reactions and to do things differently. This is what is meant by stalking oneself.

Medicine, from the angle of relationships, is the art of erasing personal history. By personal history, I mean the you that you think you are, and that you are constantly holding out for all to see. Your personal history is in every possible respect your self-image. But unless you can change that self-image, you are never going to have the freedom to be anything other than your behaviour! And that, in turn, will mean that you will never get in touch with the real you behind all of that behaviour which is being brought about because of your social conditioning. Therefore see medicine in terms of healing yourself by changing your self-image.

Religion, as we discussed before, is the art of relating to your true self, but always in the context of the world at large. Religion is therefore at the very core of all possible relationships, and in this respect has everything to do with what we may quite rightfully term the art of dreaming. The dreaming we are referring to here is, of course, the act of nurturing, irrespective of whether it is dreaming about the man in your life claiming his power as a male, or whether it is dreaming of Johnny getting a distinction in mathematics. The bottom line in all acts of nurturing is being able to relate to the desired goal in such a way that support becomes possible.

Science to the female is the art of intending conception. To grasp this, realise that in order to practise any of the first four arts, it is necessary for the female first of all to conceive the purpose. For example, it is simply not possible to erase your personal history if you cannot conceive the purpose for doing so. Likewise it is not possible to practise stalking anyone's behaviour, least of all your own, if you cannot conceive why this would be better than just beating others over the head with a frying pan, in order to get what you want. Therefore, to put it in a nutshell, intent is the basis of all the qualities of personal power the female is hunting for in the world "out there."

With respect to the above it will help greatly if we digress for a moment in order to look at the difference between personal power and freedom. Power, as we have already learned, is knowledge gained through experience, and therefore personal power is that knowledge we have gained through our own personal experiences. Freedom, on the other hand, is an extremely complex concept, and not one I can explain briefly. Therefore let it suffice for the purposes of this book simply to state that freedom is the product of using personal power. But that is not all. Every little bit of freedom acquired also generates more personal power, with the result that the two are like two sides of the same coin, and so are fully interactive and interdependent.

If we look at the five endeavours of the female within the outer world, we see that in order for her to be successful in those areas she needs personal power to begin with, for unless she already has a knowledge of what it is she is hunting for, her endeavours will not bring freedom. But that initial personal power can only really be gained through her endeavours within her inner or private world. Only once she has acquired sobriety, action, feeling, warmth and intent, will she have sufficient personal power to tackle the world out there in pursuit of freedom, for it is these five qualities of awareness that are termed personal power, or alternatively, the five aspects of The One Power.

Yet, in hunting for freedom, the female will gain even more personal power, for whatever she finds in the world out there she will immediately internalise and take "home" with her. This is to say that the female conceives as much in the outer world, as she does within her inner world, for the deepest possible meaning of conception is to nurture the purpose of the male in every possible respect, physically, emotionally and mentally. And here-in lies one of the deepest mysteries of the female, namely, her dual nature. To understand this, realise that it is the mother in the woman who nurtures the purpose of the male, but it is the female in her who conceives that purpose in the first place. As a result, the female is for ever swinging between those two polarities of her being, and unless the male initiates an intelligent co-operation between those two polarities, she will either become stuck in the polarity of motherhood, or she will become unstable in swinging backwards and forwards. In the next chapter we will look more closely at this concept.

CHAPTER TWENTY

The female pledge

~∞∾∞~

In our consideration of this section of the teachings, we first need to look at two extremely important concepts, namely, opening the heart, and entering the unknown. Both of these concepts pertain to feeling, and therefore the only way in which we can really work with them is to follow our gut feel.

The problem is that we have all been taught to think, but none of us have been taught how to feel, or how to listen to the heart. As a result most women's hearts are firmly closed, and the only thing they know is how to think rationally. However, life is not an intellectual exercise, but a feeling. Therefore in dealing with life itself, thinking is no good. Thinking is only good when we have to discriminate, in the process of finding direction. But, as we have already seen, once we have found that direction we have to turn within, in the sense of entering the unknown of our own inner being, in order to find there whatever we feel will serve the purpose of the male. Yet, in doing this, remember always that to enter the unknown is to enter the world of feeling which, by its very nature, is antithetical to thinking.

When learning to open the heart and listening to it, in order to be able to use our feelings properly, the most important thing is that we take responsibility for ourselves and for everything in our lives. By responsibility, I mean quite literally the ability to respond to life intelligently and wilfully, irrespective of whether this is responding to someone else, some challenge, or ourselves. In the case of the female, this means the ability to respond intelligently and wilfully in relation to the purpose of the male, for do not forget that in essence life is the spirit, that is, the male. In this respect it is also important to know that the female is, in fact, always responding to the male in one way or another, for it is impossible to live in the world and not to respond to the male impulse, that is, the impulse of life.

However, we must be very clear about what it means to respond. The word "respond" basically means the same as response, meaning "to pledge again." But be aware of the enormity of the implications here, for whenever we respond to the world around us, we respond to the male impulse, and therefore once again pledge ourselves to the purpose of the male. This then is the deeper meaning within the act of conception, namely, response, and so the act of opening the heart, for the female, means opening herself up, not only to her feelings, but also to intelligent and wilful response, that is, conception.

Every time the female opens herself up to the requirements of the male, irrespective of whether that is physically, emotionally or mentally, she conceives his purpose, and thereby will inevitably give birth to some form in one way or another. It is therefore so vital for the female to learn to discriminate with wisdom, for if she has not fully grasped the true requirements of the male, she will also not grasp his true purpose, and her conception will amount either to an abortion, or else the birth of a monstrosity. And herein lies the responsibility of the female, and it is also this responsibility that lies at the root of the old-fashioned value that prohibits a woman from engaging in sexual activity until she is married.

The way in which evolution has set it up, is that although it is not for the female to dictate to the male the course of his actions, yet it is the female's prerogative to choose the male with whom she will mate. There is never any need for the female to be a doormat, just as there is never a need for the female to respond to a purpose that is contrary to her beliefs. In other words, the female chooses her male in accordance with her own sense of what it is to be female.

Consequently, the act of discrimination in the female works in two ways. Firstly, it enables her to choose a male with whose purpose she feels compatible; and secondly, it enables her to conceive her mate's purpose accurately. It is here that the true power of the female lies, for although she cannot dictate to the male, she does have the power to dictate which male she is going to entice, to nurture and to pledge herself to.

A worthwhile digression at this point concerns an innate

characteristic of the female which is often frowned upon as being wrong, but which is in actual fact very normal and natural for the female. The characteristic I am referring to is the fierce competition that exists between all females. In order to understand this very natural trait in the female, know that what is seen as competition between males is not really competition at all, but rather a mutual striving together. Remember that the male is essentially very much at one with the spirit of man, and therefore the principle of unity is very important to him. As a result, the male is a creature that is constantly seeking companionship and camaraderie amongst other males. In this respect we can note that unless he has been well trained in giving a female due respect, a man will quite often put his male friends first and, in doing so, neglect his own wife.

Therefore true competition amongst males is not the socially conditioned kind, as, for example, in competing against someone else for the attention, for the business, or for the prize. Instead it is the camaraderie that exists between males striving to achieve their own true potential, and is therefore in the nature of mutual support, mutual encouragement and sharing. The way I like to express it is to say that males compete with each other, rather than against each other. Amongst males that competing is very much in the nature of, "If you can do it, then so can I," or, "Come on, if I can do it, then so can you."

But for the female it is very different, for the reason that she has to entice the male of her choice. If you are a true female, then you will also single out a man who has what it takes to be a real male. However, if you can spot his purpose and his worth, then so too can any other female, and until you have enticed him into accepting you as his female mirror, every other female is at liberty to try and net him first. The result? I do not believe I need to spell it out. You know exactly what I mean!

Therefore, even though you may find companionship with other women as you journey upon life, realise that two women can never be as close as two men, for the reason that the social being, that is, the tonal, is separative by nature. As a result, males have bosom buddies, whilst females have only other females competing, not with them, but against them!

Yet, do not let this worry you, for it is right the way it is. Since the female is the unknown, she is a mystery even unto herself, even though part of that mystery is the element of discrimination and of competing against. Every female is unique, and so too is her sense of purpose. Yet, until she has found a male who can materialise that purpose for her, it remains just a sensing, and therefore a mystery even unto her. But in order to find such a male the female has to compete against other females, and in the process learns to discriminate with incredible clarity and alacrity!

With respect to the element of competition, remember too that a mystery can only be a mystery if it is left as the unknown. Therefore it is wise never to reveal to your female friends your strategies, for if you do, you will come to regret it. There is nothing wrong with just talking or sharing, but in doing so you don't need to go into the sordid and gory details of your life. Thus the golden rule for the female is dare, do, and keep silent.

Returning now to the implications inherent within conception, we need to look at the real meaning of reproduction. In discussing this concept it is vital to keep in mind that all of mankind is in essence hermaphroditic, that is, both male and female. Here, remember that the male is in a very real sense the physical plane representative of the spirit, whilst the female is the physical plane representative of the tonal. Further, remember also that the evolution of awareness can only proceed unencumbered where there is true intelligent co-operation between the male and the female, and, of course, between ourselves and our own inner counterpart.

Therefore the whole purpose of creation, which includes the splitting of the sexes, is in fact the evolution of awareness, and to this end every male also has the power to create. As we already know, to create is a huge responsibility, for we can create true to the purpose of the spirit, or we can create monsters of depravity which destroy. But, as we have also already seen, it is in her ability to discriminate and to conceive that lies the true value and the role of the female.

Through the ability to respond intelligently and wilfully to the purpose of life, the female responds also to the purpose of the spirit, and ultimately also to the purpose of the male in her life. To put this another way, the responsibility of the female is both to choose a mate whose purpose is true to the purpose of the spirit, and also to reproduce that purpose accurately.

In order to understand this properly, it is important to remember that the female, or the tonal, for that matter, does not create in the true sense of the word, but provides the means

174

whereby the purpose of the spirit can be conceived, nurtured, and ultimately reproduced. However, this is very much in the nature of practice makes perfect, because the only way in which the evolution of awareness can take place, is for man to try over and over again to create the perfect state of awareness. Thus, the male and the female have to work together, the male constantly striving to create true to the purpose of the spirit, and the female constantly trying to conceive true to the purpose of the spirit. In this way they both co-operate intelligently towards bringing to birth the purpose of life, that is, the evolution of awareness.

It is this act of the ultimate intelligent co-operation that gives rise to what we term procreation. This is not only procreation at the physical level, but also procreation at the emotional and mental levels, for procreation at all three levels is essential for the evolution of awareness. Physical procreation speaks for itself, for clearly the evolution of awareness would cease if mankind had to stop reproducing itself. Likewise is procreation at the emotional and mental levels also essential, for emotional procreation is the act of intending to bring to materialisation our dreams, whilst mental procreation is the act of sharing knowledge in the pursuit of those dreams.

Part and parcel of the cycle of reproduction is menstruation, a natural function of the female body which far too many women have come to look upon as being a burden, if not a downright curse. Yet, how sad this is, for in that misconception women nowadays seldom if ever notice what a great and marvellous aspect of their own mystery this is, and therefore they quite literally mis-concept or mis-conceive what is a vital function of the female.

Menstruation, like conception and birth, takes place on all three levels of human endeavour, physically, emotionally and mentally. This is an essential function that must take place to make space for the new. If we look at physical menstruation, we see that the female only menstruates when she has not conceived. Accordingly, although the womb was prepared for conception, what was there could not be utilised, and therefore it had to be abandoned, or aborted, so as to prepare for something new to come. This is by far the most awesome aspect of the mystery of the female, for unbeknown even to herself, the true female can and does control conception. That is why sometimes she will conceive, and at other times not. Yet this is not a conscious act, but an act based entirely upon feeling.

There are several factors that affect the act of conception, but of these the most important is the feeling of safety. If the female does not feel safe to conceive, she will not fall pregnant. The feeling that it is not safe can be generated by all sorts of things, for example, that she senses the time is not right, that the male does not yet want children, that they cannot yet afford to have children, that the male is not committed to the marriage, and so on. But the bottom line is that, for whatever reason, the female can sense, at a very deep level of her being, that conception would be wrong, and therefore she unconsciously blocks it.

Of course, I am referring here to the true female, who takes full responsibility for being a female. I am not referring to women who have abandoned their responsibility in favour of irresponsibility, for women such as these fall pregnant at the drop of a hat, irrespective of whose hat it is! Having no self-respect, irresponsible females are quite happy to sleep around and to conceive any Tom, Dick or Harry's purpose, even if it is no purpose at all! In fact, for women such as these, physical conception is often a way in which to try and trap the man into some sort of a commitment.

If I have just described you, then I offer you no apology. I know the truth hurts, and that we mostly do not want to hear it, but we all have a choice as to what we do with our lives. From my perspective as a male, I cannot and will not condone what irresponsible and spoilt little boys have done to women. Instead I am offering you the clarity you need so as to rid yourself of the disrespect and the abuse that men have burdened you with, and to become once again a true female. But the choice is yours!

To return now to our discussion on menstruation and conception, we see that once menstruation has taken place, the female is again ready to conceive, not only physically, but also emotionally and mentally. To understand this, know that approximately two days prior to menstruation, during the time of menstruation, and for about two days afterwards, the female is in an altogether different frame of mind, since she has temporarily shifted into a state of awareness that is not her normal awareness. In that altered state of awareness she is capable of perceiving nuances that are ordinarily not perceived. This happens because the female is very much preparing herself for the new during the period of menstruation. But since the new is always sensed by the female long before she knows what it actually encompasses, she feels it as being in the nature of the unexpected. Therefore the new is always for the female an anticipation of the unexpected, and consequently is also frightening and confusing. As a result, the female will more often than not be very emotional, easily upset, and unless contained by a male who can and should impart to her a feeling of being safe, she will also be scattered in her thoughts. If the menstruating female does have a strong male in her life, she will use her feeling of insecurity to become hyper-alert to even the minutest little detail, and hyper-sensitive to even the most obscure nuance.

We need now to look at and consider the role of the male in conception. Naturally, it is impossible for the female to conceive if the male is practising contraception, or if she herself is forced to contracept, for whatever reason. Remember that here we are talking about conception at all three levels, physical, emotional and mental.

Although we are considering the total act of conception, and not just physical conception, it is a lot easier to grasp the role of the male if we first look at the physical process involved. If contraception is necessary, which it is within any normal marriage, it should always be the male who contracepts. It should never be the female's responsibility, irrespective of what method is being employed. The reason for this is that it is just too confusing for the female to have to contracept.

By this I am not inferring that women are dumb, or that they are incapable of putting two and two together. I am referring to the deep inner drives of the female which have absolutely nothing to do with rational thinking, but have everything to do with feeling and with being a true female. This is most clear to see in the use of the pill, for not only are the woman's bodily functions drastically changed by the constant intake of hormones, but her body is also kept in a perpetual state of confusion thanks to the false symptoms of pregnancy. What this boils down to, is that the female is expected to keep on accepting the male's sperm, but she is not allowed to conceive anything. In addition, she is constantly "pregnant," but that "pregnancy" never develops, and consequently she can also never give birth to anything!

Yet, realise that men who force this upon the females in their lives, or who encourage the females to take this upon themselves, also treat the female in exactly the same way, emotionally and mentally. Such men want to use, or more precisely, abuse, the female, and without ever intending to take the responsibility for being the male in that relationship. As a result, these men are every bit as confusing as the pill, since they are forever giving the female mixed messages which are utterly confusing. Just as such a man will make love passionately to his wife the one moment, but expect her not to conceive, so too will he embark passionately upon the idea of building a new home, only to tell her the following day that he has changed his mind. Such a man only "screws" the female physically, emotionally and mentally, until finally she is so confused that she feels "fucked up."

Obviously the easiest and most effective way for the male to exercise contraception is for him to use a condom. If he does so,

179

then the message to the female is clear, namely, "We are just playing here, and not being serious." Yet, the male must take care that in using a condom, he does not use also an emotional and mental condom, which unfortunately is so often the case. Most men today know only how to share their physical bodies. Therefore, even though such men may be excellent lovers in bed, they all too often are totally closed when it comes to having to share their emotions, their feelings, their ideas, thoughts, fears, doubts, insecurities, hopes, wishes, dreams, etc. Consequently, these men do not fertilise their females at any level, physically, emotionally or mentally, and in not allowing for conception to take place, these men then wonder why the female does not support them, and why she cannot bring to birth the wishes and the dreams he has never shared with her!

Therefore it is very much the male's responsibility to prescribe contraception, and how and when he will exercise it. Just as it is the male who produces the life-giving sperm, or contracepts it, so too is it he who also fertilises the female at an emotional and mental level, or denies her the opportunity to conceive his emotional stimulus and mental impulses.

When the male does take responsibility for the act of sex, as well as for the act of contraception, he will also see to it that he shares fully with the female. Knowing that it is his responsibility to show the way and to take the lead, the true male will always make quite clear to the female what is just "the exploration of potential," as opposed to what is serious, and therefore to be conceived and brought to birth. If the male does this, then the female is always amenable to exploring one thing after another in their mutual pursuit of fulfilling his purpose, for deep down inside she knows and trusts that when the male has found his direction, and pointed out the goal, he will take the lead, and by fertilising her at all levels, she will also be allowed to conceive that goal, bring it to birth, and nurture it into full materialisation. But until then, the female is also quite content to keep aborting the old in favour of the new, and even starts to regulate her menstruation. In this respect it is interesting to note how the true female who is taking the lead of a strong male, will unconsciously start to menstruate at any time of the month, simply because the male has indicated a change in direction. What an incredible ability of the female this is. Whilst many men will hold onto an outdated idea or concept for months, or even years, simply because they are too frightened to admit it will not work, the true female can drop it just like that, at a moment's notice from the male! Immediately starting to menstruate, the female is already engaged in aborting the old in preparation for the new! Phew! From a male perspective, I find that to be a truly formidable ability!

Before we leave this section, one final word of advice is called for here. Contraception practised by the male must not be seen as a license to engage in pre-marital sex, for the simple reason that sex is the act of creation, and as such should not be practised other than between husband and wife. This follows naturally from everything we have looked at so far. Leading on from this we can see that there is great validity in the old-fashioned practice of courting. During the courting, the male will do his best to capture the female's full attention, and if he is good, the female will enjoy the time spent with him enormously. But still, until such time as the male has committed himself to her in marriage, the female knows that he is only shopping around, and therefore that she cannot yet take him seriously. If she does, she will be making the fatal mistake of trying to conceive from a man who is not committed to her, and the end result will either be that he will dump her for some other girl, or he will indulge himself in the pleasures of a marriage that is not a marriage, and a commitment that is not a commitment. Having consummated a non-commitment, such a woman has only herself to thank for allowing herself to become that man's servant-whore!

CHAPTER TWENTY-ONE

Females and adaptability

❧❦❧

Adaptability plays a very important role in the life of the true female, since to adapt means to survive. But the big question that keeps coming up is how best to adapt without losing her femininity. Here it is sad to see how often the female will simply adopt the ways of men, instead of teaching herself how to adapt to them in order to survive in a male-dominated world. Therefore, the real challenge for any female is to develop enough fluidity to be able to flow with the purpose of the male, whilst still retaining her own individuality. Of course, this is quite a tall order, and not at all easy to achieve, so let us take a closer look at what this really entails.

When we look at the world today, what do we see with respect to women? On the one hand, we have those women who are the proverbial doormats, and who are nothing but second-rate citizens. These women have no real sense of self-value, and even less self-respect. They are to all intents and purposes nothing more than housekeepers and slaves to their husbands or boyfriends, whose every wish and whim is their command. Often expected to do the impossible, these women are on the whole wretched creatures leading lives of abject misery.

On the other hand, we have those women who have said enough is enough, and who have consequently stood up for their rights, and are fighting for equality and freedom. These women, like the first kind, are easily recognised, for in observing such a woman with the man in her life, it is immediately apparent who wears the pants. These are the women who have gone into competition against the males, and in doing so have established themselves very firmly in their role as the mother. To these women every male is an inadequate little boy who must be told what to do, how to do it, and when to do it. For these women it is very much a case of being better than, and "anything the male can do I can do better."

These are, of course, the two polarities, and in between these two opposites there is a whole range of women who lean towards the one polarity or the other to a greater or lesser extent. Yet, realise that in order to be a true female you cannot afford to indulge in either of these two polarities, for neither of them brings any real happiness or fulfilment.

Where the art of the true female lies, is in her amazing ability to balance the two sides of her own nature, meaning that the female must learn how to balance the mother in her with the true female, and vice versa. In other words, the female must know when to play the mother that nurtures, and when to be the female that conceives. What does this amount to in practice?

The way in which the evolution of awareness works, is that in order to bring about new knowledge we must enter the unknown, for if we don't we just remain stuck in the known. But in entering the unknown, the female invariably goes first. This is hardly surprising, considering the fact that the female is by her very nature the unknown. Therefore what is meant by "going into the unknown," is simply that the woman searches her own inner world. In doing so, the female of course encounters chaos, for remember that the unknown is chaotic until it can be brought into the ordered structure of the known. What this really means, is that the woman will see all sorts of possibilities, some of which will appear to be very good indeed, whilst others will appear to be less desirable.

However, all these possibilities, encountered by the female within the unknown of her own inner being, are merely potentials, and as such have no value in themselves unless they can be materialised in some way. But materialisation implies practical application, and obviously this entails discrimination, since before we can materialise any of these possibilities, we must first ascertain which ones will best serve our purpose.

From what we have already learned, going into the unknown is very much an act of the heart, for in working with the irrational we can only really rely upon our gut feel. However, discrimination is an act of the mind, for it means having to assess intelligently. So, in looking at what faces the female in her challenge of entering the unknown, we see that she has two options open to her. Having entered the unknown, and having seen what the possibilities are, the female can now either leave the act of discrimination and the practical application to the male, or she can simply get on with it and do it herself.

Remember that although the female must discriminate which type of male and what kind of purpose she is going to support and nurture, she must, once she has chosen her male, stand back for that male. It is therefore very much up to the male to decide what is of use to him in fulfilling his purpose, and what is not. If the female does not allow the male this decision, she will not be supporting his purpose, but will instead be trying to fulfil a purpose she is trying to superimpose upon the male.

However, great care must be taken here, for by standing back for the male, I am not in any way encouraging women to hand their power over to the male. There is a huge difference between being a doormat and a true female. The doormat type of woman pretends that she is stupid and inadequate, and therefore she makes no attempt whatsoever at being an individual in her own right. Such a woman does not even try to be a female, but simply hands over everything to her husband, including her vagina and her self-respect. For women such as these, it does not matter that they get "screwed" left, right and centre, so long as they do not have to think, or act, or take responsibility in any way. Therefore to the doormat, standing back for the male means slaving away in the kitchen, barefoot and pregnant, whilst husband is getting his rocks off with another woman who has more backbone!

In contrast, the true female will go into the unknown, but will then give all the possibilities to the male, and will allow him to make the decision as to what is the best solution. However, even when she does so, she has already first worked out all the various options for herself, and consequently cannot be bluffed or fooled by the male. It is exactly because of this that the true female will often let rip at a man who is either trying to ignore her involvement in his life, or who is simply not listening to her because he is unwilling to take the lead.

If, on the other hand, the woman decides that she can do it just as well as the male, and therefore does it all herself and of her own accord, she will be playing the role of the mother, and will end up wearing the pants. If that is her decision, then that is all fine and dandy, as long as such a woman is happy at playing the mother for the rest of her life, and is not interested in becoming a true female.

Nevertheless, it is in trying to give the possibilities to the male that most marital problems always tend to surface, for if you are sharing your life with a man who has not yet claimed his power as a male, you will find yourself in a very difficult situation. Such a man will either reject your suggestions outright, and therefore nothing you say will ever be right; or you can talk until you are blue in the face, but he will never do anything with what you try to give him! I do not believe there is a woman in the world who has not experienced this frustration at some time in her life.

But the good news about this is that it is in this challenge that the true female has the opportunity to exercise the mystery that she is. This is because, in going first in entering the unknown, the woman is also the first to see the very many possibilities inherent within any situation in life. Men, until they have claimed their power as a male, are always one step behind, and if they are stubborn or feel threatened by the woman in any way, they will invariably be several steps behind.

As a result of this, the only thing the female can do is to play mother to the man in her life whilst teaching him to grow up, so that he can claim his power as a male. This is the only way, for it is only once the man has become a true male that the woman can become a true female. So, if you are not lucky enough to find a real male, then you have no option other than to mother the man in your life into becoming a real male. But in doing so, you will have to stalk him into it. If you do it in too overt a fashion, the man will fight you with everything he has, and will more than likely end up dumping you with no thanks at all! So much then for gratitude! And so much then for women who think they can teach a man to become a male!

To understand this, you should always bear in mind that although you can mother the man in your life, in the sense of nurturing him and his purpose, you will never be able to teach him how to be male, any more than a fish can teach a bird to fly! However, by nurturing the man's ability to discriminate, he will in time begin to discriminate, and then by nurturing his desire for materialisation, you will be able to push him gently in the right direction and, once again in time, he will begin to anchor for both of you upon the physical plane. Remember, easy does it! Push the lion too hard and he will roar! Push the lion too fast and he will eat you!

What all of this really boils down to is the need for the female to be the mother in guiding the male to the vision of his own strength, potential and purpose, and then for her to evoke within him the desire to meet that vision. But once that has been accomplished, the mother must immediately step back, allow the male to make the decision, to take the lead and, above all, to take the action. At that moment the woman goes from being the mother to being the female, and in having guided the man into his maleness, she must be ready to take his lead, to accept his "sperm," and to conceive and support his purpose now that he has taken charge and set the pace.

Every true female who has ever done this will tell you that it is not only a thankless task at first, but also one that is not at all easy. This is not because it really is difficult, but merely because men are essentially rather dumb creatures. This does not imply that they lack intelligence, but rather that this is the way in which evolution proceeds. To understand this, remember that the male represents the spirit upon the physical plane, but to begin with he simply does not know what this entails, or how to go about materialising the purpose of the spirit. It is therefore very much up to the female to go into the unknown in order to find there something which will inspire in the male a sense of who and what he is, and also what his purpose in life is. Then, by using her gifts as the mother, she must guide him into accepting that vision for himself, and nurture in him the desire to become a true male. But having done this, the female must step back and allow the male to discover for himself what it really means to be male, and how to claim his power as such.

However, it is this last part that is so very difficult for the mother in the female, for, as every woman knows only too well, in the beginning the man will, like any little boy, fumble terribly in the process of learning. And consequently, time and again she will be forced either to turn a blind eye to his ineptness, or to step in as the mother to salvage what can easily become a disaster. When she does step in she gets no thanks at all, but rather, if anything, a lecture on always wanting to wear the pants!

Yet, realise that there is in fact no other way. Sometimes, as in dealing with any little boy, the mother in the female will surface, wanting to salvage something she holds dear to herself, and although this is good and right when dealing with her son, she must not make the mistake of looking upon her husband as being the same as her son. Although admittedly many men can behave remarkably like little boys, the fact remains that they are adult men and not little boys! So if the mother in the female comes out, and she wants to tell the male what to do, he cannot help but feel terribly stupid and inadequate. As a result he will also lose a great deal of self-respect and self-confidence, unless the female learns how to step back for the male.

If it is absolutely necessary to step in as the mother, simply because you feel that otherwise everything can be lost, then by all means do so, but know that it will cost you and the male in your life. Therefore think and consider very, very carefully before you choose to step in and resume the reins, even if this is only for a short time. Remember that whenever you do step in, you cut the male's legs out from under him and, depending upon his strength as an individual, it could take him years to learn to stand up again.

From everything we have learned up to this point, you, as the female, should now be able to see that there is absolutely no point in blaming the male for his lack of knowledge, or for his ineptness. Instead you should concentrate upon getting to know each of your two aspects, that is, the mother and the female, inside out, and, in doing so, learn how best to use these to your advantage.

Therefore the real struggle for survival is not so much a question of how to survive in the world of the male, but in how to survive the challenge of adapting to the needs of the male. This means that the female must learn how to adapt without losing her femininity, something which is only possible with discipline, which means self-discipline.

CHAPTER TWENTY-TWO

The journey ahead

I n this little book I have pointed you in the right direction. Now it is up to you to take what you have learned here and to use it in helping you find your way through life as a female. If you do this, you will find that the information you have been given will start to open up new areas of experience for you, and that experience will be new knowledge gained, meaning new power gained.

Take it one step at a time, and I can promise you that it will not take you long before you will start to live that new knowledge. This is what is meant by claiming your power. No-one can do this for you. Only you can claim your power.

In learning to claim your power, you will begin to learn what it is to be a true female. How much you learn will depend upon how much power you are capable of claiming. If you manage to claim only a little power, you will also gain only a little knowledge of what it is to be female, but if you claim much power, you will learn much about being female.

I cannot tell you how long it will take you, or how much you are going to learn or achieve, for this is entirely up to you. As a representative of the tonal upon the physical plane, you must never forget that there is no manual on the evolution of awareness. Just as the spirit has to write its own manual as it goes along, so too must the male in your life also learn to write his own manual. That manual will also be your manual, for remember that the purpose of the male should be the purpose of the spirit of man and, in this respect, it is also your purpose.

The nature of that manual, and how well the male in your life writes it, is dependent upon four factors. Firstly, your ability to discriminate the true purpose of the spirit; secondly, your ability to entice the right male with the right purpose; thirdly, your ability to guide that male to the vision; and fourthly, your ability to step back, so as to allow the man to claim his power as a male. Once this has been accomplished, then the male will begin to write the manual, and will begin to guide you towards your full potential as a female. But only then.

The biggest responsibility of all, and which rests squarely upon the shoulders of every true female, is that, being a representative of the tonal, she cannot plead ignorance, meaning that she cannot ever say, "I don't know how." All of us come into this life not knowing how, but then slowly but surely it begins to dawn on us, that if we don't find out how, we will die in ignorance.

The only thing we really have to do, is to open ourselves up to the world around us. The world is feminine, and the Great Mother of all is always willing to teach us, to show us the way, provided that we are willing to open our hearts to her and to heed her guidance. Let your vision of the purpose of the spirit be based upon that which our Great Mother teaches us all. In other words, as a female, you must cultivate the ability to respond to life sufficiently, to draw from it what you will need in your quest for femininity.

I have sketched for you a map of the terrain which many a female before you has already crossed, and if you use that map wisely, it will help you greatly. But realise that, as a female, you must now plan your own quest, and choose your own direction. In this respect your sense of purpose will help you. Therefore believe in your vision of that purpose and, above all, believe in yourself, for at the end of the day, that belief is all you have.

Along the way you will find other women on the same quest, and when you do find these, walk together for as long as your paths coincide, for in that companionship you will learn much from each other. However, remember always that females are in competition against each other, and therefore if you intend to be successful in your quest, then as a female you will find that you may even be forced to compete against your best friend. This is the way in which evolution has set it up, and therefore do not let it concern you. Further, remember also that the female is the unknown, and so is a mystery even unto herself. Yet, any mystery can only be a mystery if it is left as the unknown. Because of this, do not try to reveal yourself to another woman, for if you do, you will only succeed in breaking down your own intrinsic nature, and you will thereby cease to be that wonderful mystery which is the true essence of being female. So talk and share as much as you feel the need to do so, whilst always bearing in mind that the golden rule for the female is, dare, do, and keep silent.

THE QUEST FOR MALENESS

Where have all the heroes gone?

In today's world men everywhere are becoming weaker and more impotent as women challenge them in every field. What can men do about this?

Revealing the true nature of masculinity, *The Quest for Maleness* shows men how to get back in touch with the essential core of their maleness – a core that is nothing less than the untapped power of creativity. It describes how to access and release the creative power that is the right and duty of every true male to exercise. The author shows how, by doing this, you will find the wisdom, vision and sense of purpose to be a true leader, and to stand proud in your masculinity.

The Quest for Maleness is both a message of hope and a guidebook for every man who wants to find his way as a male and walk tall in the world today.

THIS DARNED ELUSIVE HAPPINESS

Théun Mares in this book shows that our most natural instinct is to be happy and fulfilled. What gets in the way is our social conditioning.

Taking us on a journey in which he explores such issues as the underlying differences between males and females, Théun reveals how we can use these to achieve new knowledge, intelligent co-operation and harmony out of conflict. He explains how we can rediscover the essential skills of passage and come to a new understanding of everything we have learned about life, our relationships with other people, our gender, and especially ourselves.

More than anything else at the moment, people are seeking answers to life and relationships. This book presents practical and down-to-earth solutions in response to this growing need. It explains that we cannot handle our relationship issues in isolation. They need to be addressed in the context of how we relate in all areas of our lives.

INSTITUTE FOR THE STUDY OF MAN

Practical courses and workshops.

Elizabeth Schnugh is director and founder of the Institute for the Study of Man, which provides practical courses based on the Toltec approach to life.

Her ten-year experience as financial director of a large multi-national company convinced Elizabeth that a radical change was needed in the ways we do things, as well as in the ways in which we relate to each other, and life in general.

She has worked closely with Théun over the past few years to design and present a series of courses with the emphasis on providing people with tools with which to uplift themselves and to change their lives. In addition to her courses for adults, she also runs weekend camps and courses for teenagers.

Elizabeth says: "The bottom line for every single person is to believe that they do have the answers for themselves. We teach people to address the issues in their lives from where they originate, rather than treating the symptoms. What this boils down to is handling relationships, for at the end of the day, all of life is about relationships. We give people practical tools to transform all types of relationships, and we address them at all levels."

For further details, as well as information on organising courses in your country, please contact:

INSTITUTE FOR THE STUDY OF MAN
PO Box 2294, Clareinch 7740, Cape Town, South Africa
Telephone: +27 21 683 5892
Fax: +27 21 683 0084
E-mail: elizabeth@toltec-foundation.org
Website: www.uplift.co.za

THE TOLTEC TEACHINGS SERIES BY THÉUN MARES

This series of books provides a more technical background to the concepts introduced in this book. Toltec means "a man or woman of knowledge," and the Toltec tradition developed as a practical approach to life, focusing on practical issues that arise in our everyday lives. This is because the only true knowledge is that which we gain from our own lives, out of our own life experience. Gaining our own knowledge implies that we are taking full responsibility for our lives, and since it is not easy to take such full responsibility, this tradition has also become known as the Warrior's Path.

Although the core truths of the Toltec tradition can be found hidden within all true religions, the Warrior's Path is not a religious or spiritual practice. Nevertheless, through developing your awareness, and by learning to see the interconnectedness of all life, you will begin to experience the underlying unity, as well as the essential truths that lie at the heart of all of the great belief systems.

BOOKS:
VOL 1: RETURN OF THE WARRIORS
VOL 2: CRY OF THE EAGLE
VOL 3: THE MISTS OF DRAGON LORE
VOL 4: SHADOWS OF WOLF FIRE (June 2000)

REVIEW COMMENTS:
- *Conscious Living – Australia* – "Without a shadow of a doubt, this book's clarity offers a wide path to intellectual freedom, spiritual joy and utter personal power."
- *Napra ReView – USA* – "This is deep, intense, rewarding material, ultimately leading to the achievement of true freedom and empowerment."

READER COMMENTS:
- "The work is clear, well-written and highly-informative."
- "... I have begun to apply practical techniques to every moment of my life. Already, only after several months, I have noticed subtle, and yet for me, dramatic effects."
- "the path of this philosophy is useful in my daily life and is not escapist in any way."

ORDERING OUR BOOKS:

Order our books from your favourite bookstore.

Alternatively, detailed ordering information, as well as online purchase
options, can be found on our websites: www.elusivehappiness.com
and www.toltec-foundation.org

For direct sales in the USA, call toll-free: 1-888-822-6657

For direct sales in England and neighbouring areas call:
Telephone: +44 1825 723398
Fax: +44 1825 724188

Otherwise please contact us directly.
Lionheart Publishing, Private Bag X5, Constantia 7848
Cape Town, South Africa

Telephone: +27 21 794 4923
Fax: +27 21 794 1487
E-mail: lionheart@toltec-foundation.org
Web: www.toltec-foundation.org and www.elusivehappiness.com

Come and visit our website for interesting articles,
new insights into handling life and relationships,
as well as online advice and sharing
of experiences in our discussion forum.